EVERYONE *Leaves*

The Strength of One Child Surviving Unthinkable Loss

LAURA IANNARELLI

CONTENTS

In loving memory of my mother, Laura Walker Iannarelli, who was taken from this world far too young. Her absence left an irreplaceable void, and my hope is that this story of death may help others to survive.

ACKNOWLEDGMENTS

I would like to thank my children, who fill my life with joy and who have exemplified my strength to never give up. My dear friend Angelica, who spent hours listening to repeated synopses as I talked through things while writing. My sister Haylee, who offered support and answered my questions along the way. My husband, who never complained about the long hours I spent writing. And Claire, my editor, whose encouragement and guidance were invaluable. I couldn't have done it without any of you.

Author Bio

Laura Louise Iannarelli endured a lifetime of torment after her mother was violently taken from her when she was seven years old. Laura went on to earn a Master's degree in counseling, is raising a beautiful, well-loved family of her own, and started a nonprofit organization, Harbor Momentum, that focuses on keeping families, specifically siblings, together. Through sharing her story, others facing traumatic situations can find their inner strength to persevere.

Disclaimer

This is a memoir. The events are portrayed to the best of the author's memory. While all of the stories in this book are true, some names and identifying details have been changed to protect the privacy of the people involved.

MY SHATTERED WORLD

"I won't cry!"

I pleaded as I sat on the couch at my uncle's house with one of my brothers and one of my sisters. The room around us was old and plain but welcoming, a place where you would snuggle up with a blanket. It was small, but in that moment, it seemed so big; the walls were white, making the room seem larger than it actually was. It was quiet, as I couldn't hear anything that was happening around me; I was zoned in on my siblings, Brian and Lisa. I had never seen them so serious, so intense. They had a secret that they wouldn't tell me. So, I sat with them, pleading back and forth; I wanted to know too.

At seven years old, I was the youngest of ten children. Leonardo, Ricardo, Jason, Tommy, and the twins, Sophia and John, were from my dad's first marriage. Haylee, Brian, Lisa, and I were from my mom and dad's marriage. In that moment, only the three of us siblings were at the house: me, Brian, and Lisa.

I persistently continued my plea. Occasionally, I would break my engrossment with them to glance around to see if anybody was coming into the room who might provide me with a hint as to what was going on; no one ever did.

"You will cry," Lisa said.

I insisted, "I promise I won't."

Brian and Lisa continued to bicker about whether or not they should let me in on their secret. I was diligent that nothing they could say could possibly make me cry.

The adults were in the other room with the television on. I'm assuming it was my Uncle Vincent, Dad's brother, and two of his adult children, Tommy and Fred. I could hear mumblings but couldn't make out what they were saying.

"Mom is dead."

I don't remember which one of them gave in and told me.

"Mom is dead."

The room started to close in on me; my eyes squinted with confusion. My mind was foggy; I couldn't think straight. I was frozen in that moment as I struggled to comprehend what was happening. Nothing seemed real. I became jittery, and my stomach turned to knots. So many questions were racing through my mind. What did they mean she was dead? How could that be? How did they know? What does it even mean to be dead?

For the previous three years of my life, I had been constantly uprooted. When I was four years old, Mom left the abusive life she faced at the hands of Dad and took us kids with her. Dad found out where we were and stole us back to live with him; Mom then made a plan to steal us back from Dad, and over and over again. It was like tug of war, and we, Brian, Lisa, Haylee, and I, were the rope.

I remember one time when we were at our house with Dad, Haylee took me for a walk. I couldn't wait to go for the walk; I had been nagging her all day to take me. Our two-story house was on a back country road, away from the hustle and bustle of the towns but close enough to other houses that we weren't secluded. It sat slightly back off the road, leaving a small front yard for us to play in. There was a creek that ran behind it that flowed parallel to the road. We walked down the street, over a little bridge, then past the one-man-sized house on the corner. We turned onto another road and walked up the big hill. I felt happy with Haylee, happy that she had taken the time to walk so far with me. We were taking our time, not rushing to get back, just enjoying the time together. Once we got to the top of the hill, Aunt Shirley, Mom's sister, pulled up and stopped. My heart sank when I saw her. I knew immediately what that meant; she was there to take us back to Mom. I didn't want to go with Mom; she wasn't as fun as Dad. As fast as I could, I took off running down the hill, racing back toward Dad. I barely got started when Haylee grabbed my arm and stopped me. Her grip was strong, authoritative, and intense. I couldn't get away. She put me in the car, and we sped off. I cried. I cried so hard; I didn't want to leave Dad. I never wanted to leave Dad.

Another time, when we lived in Alabama with Mom, Dad showed up, completely unexpectedly. I was always ecstatic when this happened. I couldn't contain my excitement. My first thought was always me hoping that I would get to leave with him. I've been told that he was lost without us kids and that he would look for us diligently. Then, when he would learn of our approximate location, he would go to the town he expected us to be in and would just walk the sidewalks or drive around the streets until he found us.

On that day, I remember getting into the car with him while Brian and Lisa were running on the road in front of us, guiding his car to our apartment, waving their arms as if to say, "Come on," while Dad and I drove slowly behind them. This happened while Mom was at work, so she knew nothing about it. I don't remember Haylee being home either. Sure enough, just as I wanted, he stole us back. We piled up into the car, and he took us back to Pennsylvania to live with him.

During those three years, I lived in Pennsylvania, Alabama, Texas, and then moved back to Pennsylvania.

On this day, though, the most life-altering day of my existence, Brian, Lisa, and I were with Dad, and Haylee was with Mom.

Earlier in the day, Brian, Lisa, and I had been at Uncle Vincent's house visiting. Dad came to pick us up to take us home. He was drunk, as usual, but nobody ever seemed to be too concerned about this, nor was anybody concerned about us going in the car with him in that condition. We lived about a mile and a half away. I didn't want to go home yet, so Uncle Vincent let me stay with him. I loved being with Uncle Vincent. He was such a nice man. He spoke kindly and softly. He showed he cared through both his actions and his words. His house was always clean, and there was always food, all of which illuminated a strong sense of comfort for me. Most desirable was that I always knew what to expect when I went there; nothing changed. In the midst of all the turmoil I was living in, the back and forth between homes, the fighting between Mom and Dad, the never knowing what was next, his home offered stability. Plus, he let me eat all the ice cream I could ask for.

Uncle Vincent

Dad left with Brian and Lisa. In retrospect, I realize that was the last time I saw Dad. At the time, I didn't think of it that way, of course. I had no idea that I would never see him again; you never think the last time will be the last time until it's over. I was just happy that he let me stay with Uncle Vincent.

When Dad, Brian, and Lisa pulled up to our house, the yard was swarming with people, including police officers. Brian and Lisa were immediately rushed off to the neighbor's house. Mom's fiancé, Joe, was one of the people there. Apparently, Mom was living with Joe at the time.

That morning, she had gone to see Dad, which is probably why Brian, Lisa, and I were staying at Uncle Vincent's. When she didn't show up for work or return home later that day, Joe began to worry and went looking for her. He said he had seen Dad's station wagon parked beside the house earlier, and later, while searching for Mom, he came across her van abandoned in an empty parking lot about a mile down the road. Once he noticed that Dad had left the house, he went back there and started looking around.

He found a pile of dirt with tires on it beside the house, next to the well. He removed some of the dirt and found feet sticking up out of the ground. It was Mom. Mom had been buried in a hole beside our well and then covered with dirt and tires.

Buried… in a hole!

Joe called the police.

As Dad got out of his car, he went to talk to the police. Joe told the police that Dad had killed Mom, while Dad just stood there. Dad also told the police that he killed her, that he shot her in the kitchen. Dad was taken away to jail.

I don't remember when or how I found out these details, but I remember the immediate feeling of numbness, of disbelief; I couldn't imagine it was true. I kept trying to make sense of it all. The confusion only intensified. Dad killed Mom.

Dad killed Mom!

Dad buried Mom in a hole!

My heart stops for a moment every time I hear those words, even to this day; it's like I'm shocked all over again.

I think about this as an adult. I imagine the additional trauma that Brian and Lisa and I would have faced, if I hadn't stayed at Uncle Vincent's, had we walked into the house and seen the mess of what had transpired there. Why would Dad take us kids back to that house? Was he going to carry on as if nothing had happened? What was he thinking? Was he thinking? I'm thankful as an adult that I was not there, and that Brian and Lisa did not go inside that house.

So, there I sat on the couch. The secret was out; I was trying to understand, to process, what it actually meant for someone to be dead. What it meant to never see Mom again.

After a few moments, I ran into the living room with the adults. I saw Bullet, our dog, a beautiful white German Shepherd, on the television. He was running back and forth outside our house. He carried the weight of the chain to which he was attached back and forth, over and over again, while he barked, presumably upset with all the commotion that was going on there. I wonder what happened to Bullet.

That's all I remember seeing on the television. One of the adults said they wanted to "watch it one more time," then they turned it off. I've always wondered why they wanted to "watch it one more time." Did they think they missed something? Were they in disbelief too? Were they just trying to process what they were seeing? I don't know why, but it never sat well with me that they wanted to see it again.

I think we left the house at that point, although I don't remember if we actually did or not. If we did, I have no idea where we went.

Oh, and I did cry. Brian and Lisa were right.

Husband charged in wife's murder

Frank Charles Iannarelli, 53, of Shenango Township was charged last night with first degree murder in connection with the death of his wife.

The body of Kathy Iannarelli, 33, was found buried in a shallow grave at 8 p.m. yesterday beside Iannarelli's residence on Union Valley Road.

Mrs. Iannarelli of Portersville was reportedly last seen alive yesterday about 8 a.m. She died of a gunshot wound.

A NEIGHBOR said a friend of Mrs. Iannarelli and another man started searching for the woman when she failed to show up for work yesterday. The neighbor could not identify either man.

The two men arrived at the Iannarelli house, which was vacant at the time, to continue the search. They looked around the house and discovered fresh dirt with tires thrown on top beside the building.

The neighbor said they started digging through the dirt and uncovered the victim's foot. The victim's friend then ran to a nearby residence to call the state police.

AFTER CALLING police, the neighbors returned to the scene with the victim's friend. They said they saw Iannarelli in a car with two children and asked him what happened. Iannarelli reportedly said he did not know.

State police arrested Iannarelli and took him to be arraigned before District Magistrate Betty Lou Kradel. He was charged with first degree murder and committed to Lawrence County Jail. He was held without bail.

State police are continuing the investigation and are being assisted by Shenango Township Police.

8|13|80

Wampum Man Held For Murder of Wife From Portersville Area

A Wampum man was charged with the murder of his wife from the Portersville area, after her body was discovered last night covered with dirt alongside the back porch of his residence on Union Valley Road, in Shenango Township, Lawrence County.

Dead is Laura Lee Iannarelli, 33, of Portersville. Police said an autopsy was being performed this morning by Lawrence County Coroner Howard Reynolds to determine the cause of her death.

Frank Charles Iannarelli, 53, of Wampum R.D. 1, is charged with the murder of his wife. He was arraigned before District Magistrate Betty Lou Kradel and lodged in the Lawrence County Jail without bond.

According to New Castle State Police, Mrs. Iannarelli's body was found covered with dirt alongside the back porch of her husband's residence on Union Valley Road. Police, who estimated the time of death between 8 and 9 p.m. Tuesday, divulged no further information.

State Police are continuing the investigation with assistance from the Shenango Township Police Department.

Wampum Man's Wif[e]
Died of Multiple Gu[n]
Wounds, Coroner Ru[les]

Multiple gunshot wounds have [been] determined as the cause of death [of a] Wampum area man's wife, whose [body] was found Tuesday night covered [in] dirt alongside the back porch of [his] home on Union Valley Road, in [She]nango Township, Lawrence County.

The estranged husband, Fr[ank] Charles Iannarelli, 53, Wampum R.[D.], is being held for murder.

The body of Laura Lee Iannarelli[, 34] of Portersville, was found by her [boy]friend, ______________, part[ly] buried beneath tires, plywood and [dirt] in Iannarelli's yard. ______ told [po-]

Continued on Page 2. Col. 1

Wampum Man's Wife

★ From First Page

lice he became concerned when she failed to return home after visiting her estranged husband to discuss problems about Ianarelli's four children who lived with her.

______ reportedly went to the Ianarelli's residence and saw a foot sticking from the ground in a sunken area of the yard, and notified police.

Lawrence County Coroner Howard Reynolds said Wednesday that the victim died of multiple gunshot wounds to her chest.

Iannarelli was arraigned before District Magistrate Betty Lou Kradel on a charge of criminal homicide, and committed to the Lawrence County Jail without bond.

Police estimated the time of Mrs. Iannarelli's death between 8 and 9 p.m. Tuesday.

State Police are continuing the investigation with assistance from the Shenango Township Police Department.

Mrs. Iannarelli's body was taken to the Edward A. DeCarbo Funeral Home in New Castle.

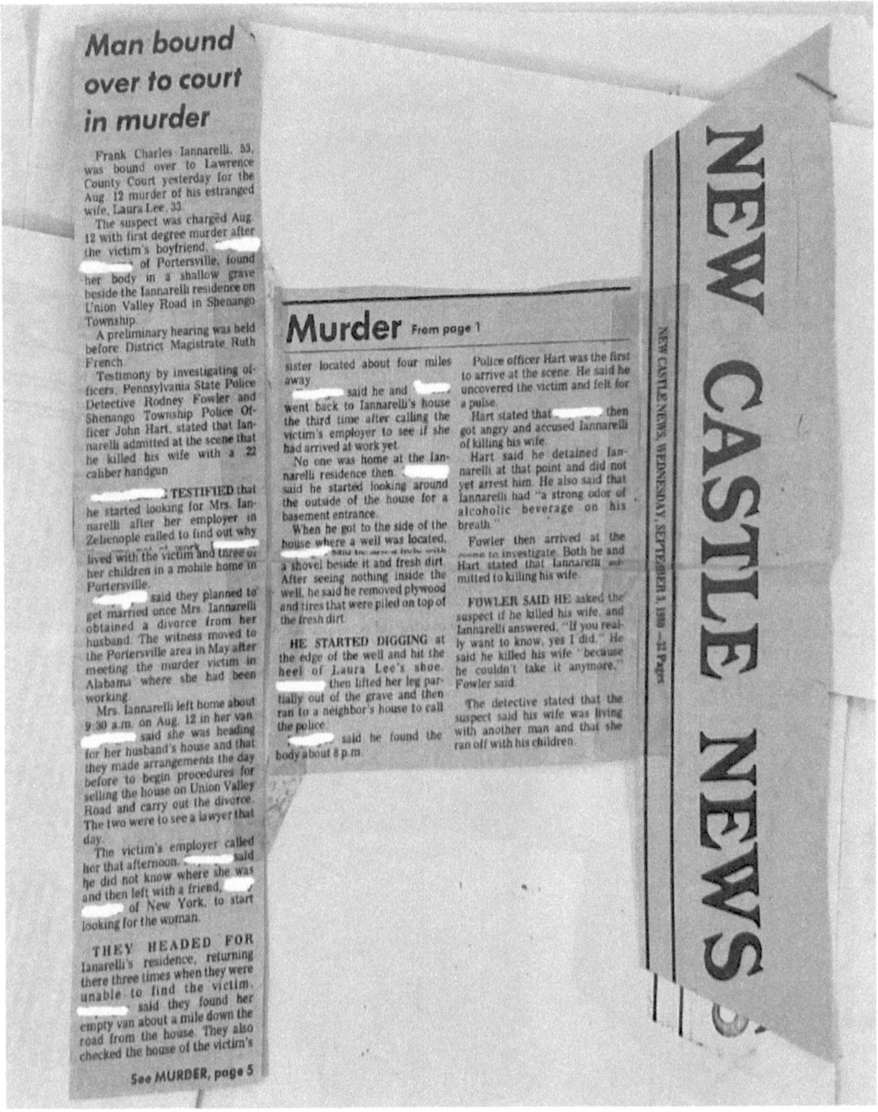

Man bound over to court in murder

Frank Charles Iannarelli, 53, was bound over to Lawrence County Court yesterday for the Aug. 12 murder of his estranged wife, Laura Lee, 33.

The suspect was charged Aug. 12 with first degree murder after the victim's boyfriend, ——— of Portersville, found her body in a shallow grave beside the Iannarelli residence on Union Valley Road in Shenango Township.

A preliminary hearing was held before District Magistrate Ruth French.

Testimony by investigating officers, Pennsylvania State Police Detective Rodney Fowler and Shenango Township Police Officer John Hart, stated that Iannarelli admitted at the scene that he killed his wife with a 22 caliber handgun.

——— TESTIFIED that he started looking for Mrs. Iannarelli after her employer in Zelienople called to find out why ——— lived with the victim and three of her children in a mobile home in Portersville.

——— said they planned to get married once Mrs. Iannarelli obtained a divorce from her husband. The witness moved to the Portersville area in May after meeting the murder victim in Alabama where she had been working.

Mrs. Iannarelli left home about 9:30 a.m. on Aug. 12 in her van. ——— said she was heading for her husband's house and that they made arrangements the day before to begin procedures for selling the house on Union Valley Road and carry out the divorce. The two were to see a lawyer that day.

The victim's employer called her that afternoon. ——— said he did not know where she was and then left with a friend, ——— of New York, to start looking for the woman.

THEY HEADED FOR Iannarelli's residence, returning there three times when they were unable to find the victim. ——— said they found her empty van about a mile down the road from the house. They also checked the house of the victim's

See MURDER, page 5

Murder From page 1

sister located about four miles away.

——— said he and ——— went back to Iannarelli's house the third time after calling the victim's employer to see if she had arrived at work yet.

No one was home at the Iannarelli residence then. ——— said he started looking around the outside of the house for a basement entrance.

When he got to the side of the house where a well was located, ——— said he saw a hole with a shovel beside it and fresh dirt. After seeing nothing inside the well, he said he removed plywood and tires that were piled on top of the fresh dirt.

HE STARTED DIGGING at the edge of the well and hit the heel of Laura Lee's shoe. ——— then lifted her leg partially out of the grave and then ran to a neighbor's house to call the police.

——— said he found the body about 8 p.m.

Police officer Hart was the first to arrive at the scene. He said he uncovered the victim and felt for a pulse.

Hart stated that ——— then got angry and accused Iannarelli of killing his wife.

Hart said he detained Iannarelli at that point and did not yet arrest him. He also said that Iannarelli had "a strong odor of alcoholic beverage on his breath."

Fowler then arrived at the scene to investigate. Both he and Hart stated that Iannarelli admitted to killing his wife.

FOWLER SAID HE asked the suspect if he killed his wife, and Iannarelli answered, "If you really want to know, yes I did." He said he killed his wife "because he couldn't take it anymore," Fowler said.

The detective stated that the suspect said his wife was living with another man and that she ran off with his children.

CHAPTER TWO

THE FUNERAL

The next I-don't-know-how-many days are a blur for me. I remember being at the funeral home. I don't remember who took me there or if any of my brothers or sisters arrived with me. I remember walking up to the huge brick building, wanting to hurry and get inside, though I had no idea what to actually expect once I got there. I remember that a stoic-looking man held the door for me as I entered. He wore a nicely pressed suit, and his face had no expression. He guided me down the hall to the room where my mom was. I looked around, trying to make sense of my surroundings. The room was huge, cold, quiet, and unwelcoming. Soft music played from the ceiling, and it was filled with rows of chairs, with people occupying many of them, some socializing, some crying, some laughing with each other.

Then I saw Mom. She was lying in a coffin at the front of the room, and from where I was standing, she seemed so far away.

I stood still. I took deep breaths in and out as I zoned in on her. The rest of the room, the people, the soft music, the stoic man, no longer existed to me. I went to her. She was wearing a pretty pink dress; pink was her favorite color, and the dress had a brooch on it. Her hair and makeup were neatly done, and her hands were folded at her waistline. She was surrounded by flowers and covered with a clean white blanket. I stared at her. In that moment, it was just me and Mom. I couldn't hear anything, feel anything, smell anything, or even see anything except Mom. The knot in my stomach was still there from when I learned of her death, but now it tightened. A weight landed on my shoulders. I wanted to touch her, to pinch her so she would wake up, look at me, and smile, but I just stared. I imagined this wasn't real, that it was just a bad dream. I tried to wake myself up from it, but I couldn't.

I felt disbelief, intense sadness, and a profound emptiness. I continued to wait for her to sit up. She didn't. I didn't truly grasp the absoluteness of her death, of this goodbye, but I knew I would never see her alive again.

The next thing I remember is that I was sitting on someone's lap. They told me it was okay to cry. I told them I had already cried, then I got off their lap and away from them. Who were they to give me that kind of permission anyway? Even on that day, at that young age, I remember thinking that even though I didn't want to be around whoever that was, I knew I didn't really have anybody to run to. The harsh realization was sinking in, and fast.

Mom was gone, forever. Dad was gone, probably forever. I was only seven years old. I hadn't had stability in my life for at least the past three years, and now everything had taken another significant turn. I was sad, confused, and unsure, but I wasn't afraid.

In that moment, with the sadness, confusion, and discontentment in me and surrounding me; with the history of turmoil, the history of tug-of-war, the history of uncertainty, and the current status of being in the midst of chaos, I learned that I couldn't be afraid. I learned that I just had to deal with what was going on, stand strong, and persevere. I had to sit back and see how the grown-ups were going to handle this, and I had to find out where I was going to live now that I, all of a sudden, no longer had parents.

CHAPTER THREE

THE MOVE

Mom was gone, and Dad was in jail. My next steps had been decided. I don't remember the move or know how it came about. I don't know if anybody asked me where I wanted to live. I don't know if I had any input at all. I don't remember conversations, whispers in hushed tones, packing my belongings, or anything of the sort. I don't even know who was making all of the decisions for me. All I know is that I was moved to Michigan to live with my oldest sister, Sophia, and her husband, John.

It was Sophia, John, and their kids, Steve and Nicole. Steve was the same age as me; Nicole was just a baby.

John, Sophia, Nicole, Steve, Laura (me)

Sophia was always so nice to me; she took good care of me. I have pictures from when I lived with her. My hair was always nicely kept, and my clothes were always clean.

Laura

Laura w/Santa

My 8ᵗʰ Birthday

I rarely had clean clothes before that. When I lived with Mom and Dad, my sister Haylee would sometimes wear her clothes backward so that the clean side would be in the front, so nobody would see that they were actually dirty. I appreciated the clean clothes.

At the time, I was confused by it all, though. I remember thinking I didn't belong there, that this was "high-class," and that I'd be in some serious trouble if I got my clothes dirty or, worse, if I couldn't adjust to this new way of living. I also remember feeling uneasy because I had nothing to compare it to. I wanted to fit in with my new family but didn't really know how to do that. I carried the weight of feeling like I was supposed to have all the answers already. Of course, I never told anyone I felt like this, so I carried it alone and therefore tried to handle it alone. I had it in my mind that I didn't need anybody's help.

I spent my second-grade school year there, in Michigan. I'm not sure I remember my teacher's name now. I think it was Mrs. Brueck, but I remember that her birthday was one day after mine. I felt like I had a connection with her because of the coincidence. She was very sweet. She gave me a hug at the end of every day. She might say that it was me giving her a hug, but whatever.

I remember when I learned to ride a bike. Sophia let me take Steve's bike down the street while she and John watched. They were watching because they were proud of me for learning how to do it. I turned around in the neighbor's driveway, where Sophia had specifically told me not to turn around because it was a gravel driveway.

Sure enough, I put a hole in one of the bike tires. She and John were mad at me, but they didn't beat me. I remember being surprised about that because I was used to seeing people get beaten when they didn't listen, or for no reason at all.

I remember Sophia clipping my toenails. I couldn't stand it, but of course, it was necessary. I just couldn't stand her touching my feet, and I was thoroughly convinced that she was going to miss the nail and clip my toe. She never did.

Another thing I remember about living with Sophia is that I wanted a cat. Sophia wouldn't let me have one, though, because she was afraid the cat would lick milk off Nicole's sweet little face.

I shared a bedroom with Steve while I lived there. One night, I woke up confused. I noticed there was a door to the right of me and another door at my feet, along the far wall. I started panicking because there was a room in my old house, where I lived with Mom and Dad, that had doors in those exact same places. I felt disoriented and became increasingly petrified as I slowly looked around the room, back and forth at the doors. It was dark, with only the shadows from the curtains showing on the walls. I could barely make out the details in the room as I tried to figure out where I was. It was the middle of the night, and it was deafeningly quiet.

The more I tried to make sense of it, the faster my heart raced and the heavier my breathing became. I knew I was at Sophia's house, but the room made me think I was back in my old house. I could not figure out my surroundings. I sat up and started screaming.

Sophia ran into the room to see what was wrong. She was quick to react, alarmed yet concerned. She threw herself beside me on the bed and hugged me tightly while caressing my hair. I'm sure she spoke, but I don't remember what she said. Her calm tone and gentle actions comforted me. I don't think either one of us got any more sleep that night.

CHAPTER FOUR

WHERE IS MY SISTER?

Brian and Lisa moved to Michigan at the same time I did. We might have all gone to Michigan in the same car at the same time, but I don't remember.

Lisa went to live with our brother Leonardo and his family. It was Leonardo, his wife Jane, and their kids, Michelle and Eric. Brian went to live with another one of our brothers, Ricardo, and his family. It was Ricardo, his wife Karen, and their kids, Denise and Kate.

The three of us, Brian, Lisa, and I, weren't living in the same house, but we weren't far from each other either. I got to see Brian and Lisa at least once a week, as we all got together for a family meal every Sunday. Seeing them was the highlight of my week, and the consistency of it relaxed me.

Laura, Lisa, Brian

I loved it there in Michigan, living with Sophia. I had stability, food, clean clothes, most of my brothers and sisters, plus my nieces and nephews. They were the same age as me; actually, some were even older than me. This was my first taste of what a healthy family unit looked like. Most importantly, I wasn't seeing adults constantly fighting like Mom and Dad had done. I felt safe, stable, accepted, and loved.

But where was Haylee? Where was my sister? Why didn't she move to Michigan with the rest of us? Nobody seemed to have any idea where she was.

Not only had I lost my mother and father, but had I lost my sister too? I missed her so much. Where was she?

CHAPTER FIVE

THE DISRUPTION OF A BLESSING

When second grade ended, my Grandpap, Mom's dad, came and took me away from Sophia and the life I had embraced and grown to love. He gathered me and all of my belongings, loaded everything into his car, and took me back to Pennsylvania.

This was another decision the adults made for me. I didn't want to leave. I wanted to stay in the nice, stable, clean home I had lived in for the past school year. But someone decided I needed to move back to Pennsylvania. I don't know who decided, but that was that.

Who knows? Maybe it was too much for Sophia and John, for Leonardo and Jane, for Ricardo and Karen. They were still young themselves, and this murder was committed by their father too. I can't imagine this was easy for them.

I think about the love they had for us; Brian, Lisa, and me. They opened their hearts and homes to three kids who had been through a whirlwind, who were dealing with a flood of emotions that nobody, not even us, could predict or understand, and yet they still offered to take us in. They gave us the best life they could, all while, I imagine, trying to maintain normalcy while raising their own kids, presumably without wanting them to feel the impact or fallout from the traumatic situation that had taken place. It couldn't have been easy for them.

Maybe I cried about being away from Pennsylvania. Maybe, even though I loved the stability, I was expressing that I wanted to go "home." I don't remember doing this, but it could have happened. And if it did, maybe they thought letting me go back was best.

Maybe Mom's family just wanted me to be with them. I learned later that they wanted me to be away from Dad's family. Maybe they thought uprooting me again would be best in the long run, that moving me back to the place I was originally from and used to being in was best. Maybe they just missed me and felt I'd been torn away from them when I moved to Michigan. Who knows?

Nonetheless, there I was, once again, being uprooted, moved from the stability and normalcy I had briefly been blessed with.

I rode in the car with Grandpap. It was just the two of us, and he let me sit in the front seat. The car was big, long and wide. Grandpap was pretty well off, so it might have been a Cadillac. The seats were soft, and the car was quiet. There was a tassel of some sort, maybe an air freshener, hanging down from the middle control knobs.

I looked up at Grandpap as he drove, making mental notes of the wrinkles on his forehead and the sideburns above his ears. He was a man of authority, a man who commanded respect, but he was gentle with me.

I was excited that he was the one who picked me up. I was excited because I thought I was going to live with him. Grandpap lived in Ohio, about a half hour away from where I lived with Mom and Dad. I loved my Grandpap. He was so nice and calm, easy to talk to. Even though I wasn't happy about leaving Michigan, I was happy to be going with him.

My excitement, however, was squashed when I found out that I actually wasn't going to live with him. Grandpap said that as much as he would love for me to live with him, that wasn't an option.

During our drive to Pennsylvania, I begged him to reconsider, to change his mind, to let all four of us kids live with him, to keep us together, but he didn't cave. After all, Grandpap had a lot going on too. He was remarried and had a wife, Sharon, and together they had a son, Mark. I was crushed. I couldn't believe he wouldn't take us in, that he didn't want us, that he didn't want me.

Grandpap thought it would be best for me to live with my Aunt Judith, my mom's sister. Now, this wasn't news that made me sad. I'm told that before my mom died, I was with Aunt Judith and her kids all the time, but I don't remember.

I do remember that I was happy to be going to live with her. She had six kids, my cousins. There was Debbie, the oldest; Michael, who was always working; Linda, the bossy one; Kevin, the quiet one who was always working on cars; Amy, who was the same age as me; and Heather, the youngest. Their house was only a couple of miles away from Uncle Vincent's house and my mom and dad's house, so I was familiar with the area. What a great place for me to live, or so I thought. After all, I was only eight years old.

Of all my cousins, I was most excited to see Amy and Heather because I wanted to play with them. They weren't home when I got there. I remember just hanging out in the living room with Aunt Judith and some other people.

I don't remember who else was there, and I don't remember talking to anyone. I just remember feeling out of place because I was the newcomer. I felt like I was all by myself, and I felt like everyone was staring at me.

When I knew that Amy and Heather were home, I hid behind the chair so I could surprise them. I heard their car doors open and close. I hadn't seen them in so long, almost a year, and I couldn't wait for them to come in. My heart pounded faster and faster with excitement. I heard their voices getting closer, then I heard them come into the house.

"Surprise!" I jumped out from behind the chair. Their jaws dropped. They were so excited to see me. We ran to each other and hugged. We were all ecstatic that I was there. I knew they would be as happy to see me as I was to see them. I felt happy inside that they were as happy as they were.

CHAPTER SIX

BEHIND CLOSED DOORS

The house I lived in with Aunt Judith was a big one. It had two stories, a large kitchen, a large living room, and four bedrooms. Amy, Heather, and I all shared a bedroom. I didn't mind it because I was happy to be with them. Plus, as much as I acted like I didn't need anybody, I didn't really like being alone.

At first, living at Aunt Judith's was fun, new, and exciting. I enjoyed being around everyone and being in another stable home. A home where I had live-in playmates, a home that was always clean, that always had food on the table, a home where I wasn't always wondering if someone was going to steal me away at a moment's notice, where I was part of a family. A home where I belonged. The environment was soothing to me and helped me be at ease. I was getting comfortable and nicely settling into my new environment.

It didn't take long, however, for those feelings to wear off. I started to get in trouble for everything, even things I didn't do. Nothing I ever did was right: I used the utensils wrong, I said the wrong things, I sat the wrong way, I chewed my food wrong, I looked at people the wrong way, I couldn't calm down, I was too fidgety, I was too needy. I felt like I was always under a microscope, with every imperfection being pointed out constantly, and often in front of everybody. I couldn't do anything right.

I started questioning myself, double-checking my actions before I spoke or even moved a muscle so I could make sure I wasn't doing things the wrong way. Of course, this technique didn't work for me because I could not understand what it was that I was doing wrong to begin with. How could I fix things that didn't seem to be broken?

Even silly things would set Aunt Judith off. We were all sitting at the dinner table one night, which was one of the nice things about living there: we always ate dinner together. My aunt served us meat with green beans. I grabbed the ketchup. As soon as I went to put it on my plate, Aunt Judith scolded me, "Don't put ketchup on your green beans." I asked her why not and told her that I always put ketchup on them. She told me that was gross and that I wasn't allowed to do that anymore.

It wasn't so much the words that were hurtful; it was her tone, as if it was sickening to ever think to do such a thing. It was the repulsed look on her face as she scolded me that cut to my core, which carried the message that *I* was disgusting. The table got really quiet. I could feel everyone looking at me as if I were defective, but nobody said anything. I was embarrassed, and I was angry at her for humiliating me. A lump formed in my throat as I quietly looked down at my plate. I didn't say anything else, though. I kept it all in.

That's what I learned to do with my emotions while living with Aunt Judith. *Who was she to decide what ketchup goes on, anyway?* I just sat there and played with my green beans. I didn't want to eat them at all now, but if I didn't, I wouldn't be allowed to get up from the table.

Now, as an adult, I think putting ketchup on green beans would indeed be gross, but as a child, I loved it. It just didn't make any sense to me why I kept getting in trouble. Why couldn't she ever speak to me nicely, like I was someone who needed to learn something and she was someone who could teach or guide me? Was there something wrong with me? I started to think that there was. I also felt perhaps I was unreasonably being compared to my cousins' mannerisms, or that maybe since I was the outsider, she could treat me as such. I couldn't figure it out.

All I knew was that the environment at Aunt Judith's house was one I was definitely not used to. I went from being in a situation where people, namely Mom and Dad, were fighting over me, literally, to this one: a situation where I had to learn how to function where I was insignificant, belittled, unheard, falsely accused, and seemingly unwanted.

I want to point out that this was definitely not my imagination. One day when Richard, Aunt Judith's boyfriend, was visiting, he witnessed the way she treated me. Aunt Judith had told us, Amy, Heather, and I, to go outside and play. None of us wanted to, but we knew we didn't have a choice. We all got up and went outside. After maybe ten minutes, Amy went back inside. A little later, Heather followed. So, there I was, outside by myself, contemplating whether or not it was okay for me to go back inside too. I waited another 15 minutes or so; they didn't come back out, so I figured it must be okay to go back inside. I quietly made my way back into the house. As soon as I sat down with everyone else, Aunt Judith looked at me and snapped, "I told you girls to go outside and play!" Everyone looked at me, and believe me, I could feel the weight of their stares, their disappointment, their accusations, all of which were blaming me for them having to go back outside. The weight of it sat heavy on me; I had messed up again.

Then something unexpected happened. Richard looked at Aunt Judith and said, "You treat her like an unwanted stepchild!" Dead silence filled the air. Our eyes got wide as we, Amy, Heather, and I, glanced at each other. Nobody ever spoke back to Aunt Judith like that. We quickly removed ourselves from the room and went back outside. I don't know exactly what happened after the door closed behind us, but I know that we didn't see Richard at the house again for a long time.

Up until the time I moved in with Aunt Judith, all things aside, I had always felt loved and wanted. This was new territory, and I was alone in it. I had to figure out how to navigate it on my own. There wasn't anybody to lean on or seek advice from because I was the outsider, and everyone knew it.

Imagine, if you will, living in a home where nothing you do is ever right. I would reluctantly walk down the stairs each morning with negative anticipation, not knowing which Aunt Judith I was going to get. Would she be happy, in a good mood, and tolerate me? Or would she be annoyed that I was there, tell me I was wearing the wrong clothes, or scold me for something insignificant? There was no in-between. I honestly cannot remember one time when we had a loving and bonding moment. It was always a degrading and humiliating correction and redirection.

I lived like this every day, the entire time I was there. Every moment of every day felt like I was walking across a landmine, never knowing when I would activate an explosion.

The punishments were new to me too. Not that I wasn't ever punished before I moved there, maybe I wasn't, I don't remember, but it was definitely different in her house. There were spankings if we didn't listen. I was used to seeing other people get spankings, such as my brothers and sisters, but I couldn't recall ever actually being the recipient. One time at Aunt Judith's, she gave me a spanking. When she left the room, I said, "That didn't even hurt," to one of my cousins. I guess she heard me because she came back with an electric cord. I never let her hear me again.

One day Aunt Judith got me new pajamas. I was so excited and appreciative. They made me feel important. They were a one-piece pajama set, long legs and long sleeves. I felt like a million dollars when I strutted into the living room to watch television with everyone else while wearing these new pajamas. I was so happy that Aunt Judith had bought these for me, that she had thought of me. When I got to the living room, I stood behind the chair she was sitting in and rested my arms on the back of it. I felt like I wanted to be close to her, as she had done something nice for me. After a few minutes, she said degradingly, "Go sit down. You're not special just because you got new pajamas." That might not seem like a big deal, but it was to me. It crushed my heart. All of those feelings of warmth and closeness I was feeling toward her instantly vanished. It reiterated to me that I was not important, and it exemplified the fact that she didn't want me near her. I wanted that connection with her, with anybody, so badly, but it just wasn't there on her end. *I felt unwanted.* An emotional coldness deepened within me, and the lump in my throat hardened as I choked back my tears. I slowly walked over to the couch and sat down.

CHAPTER SEVEN

GIVING MY ALL

There was a teenager who hung around Aunt Judith's house, and he was the only person in my life at that time who actually talked to me. Not at me, not past me. To me. He made me feel like I wasn't a defect that needed fixing. Sometimes he even thought I was funny. Spending time with him was like coming up for air after being held underwater.

Like everything else in my life at that time, before long this too took a turn.

One day he told me he wanted to show me something. We walked away from the house together, talking. I remember the sound of our footsteps on the gravel getting quieter, the voices of everyone else fading behind us. When we reached a spot where no one could see us, his whole demeanor changed. The lightness dropped from his face. He looked around to make sure nobody was near, and then he slowly pulled his pants down. Not all the way, just far enough. I was confused. I didn't understand why he was doing that or what was happening. Then he took my hand and showed me how to touch him. I was puzzled, but hesitantly, I complied.

The moment felt wrong to me, through every part of my being, but I didn't know enough to know just how wrong it actually was. When he told me I couldn't tell anybody about it, the feelings I already had were solidified, and I knew that this was not something he should be asking me to do.

In a twisted way, though, it also made me feel special. Like he had confided in me. Like he trusted me to keep his secret.

That's how confused my mind was. Nobody trusted me with anything. I was being told I was wrong about everything, abandoned by everyone, ridiculed daily. It put me in a position where I was willing to keep a secret for someone simply because he trusted me to do so. So, I did.

This was the beginning of him teaching me how to perform sex acts on him. If I didn't do something the way he wanted the first time, he would show me a different way. It made me very uncomfortable, but it made him happy, and it didn't seem like it was that big of a deal, so I just did it. I mean, I was eight years old. I didn't have much insight into what was actually going on.

I remember I would count the seconds. I would make up a number in my head and count to that number, as if somehow the number I chose would correlate with the act and it would magically end when I reached it. I just wanted to get it over with so I could go do something else.

In my mind, at that age, it seemed like a small price to pay for the attention he gave me. Nobody else was spending any time with me. I remember wondering,

Is this the kind of thing people do with their friends?

It became frequent. He would take me places to perform these acts. He would sneak into the bathtub with me. He would wake me up after I was asleep. Sometimes I would pretend to still be sleeping so I wouldn't have to engage.

This went on the entire time I lived with Aunt Judith. I hated every minute of it, but I knew I couldn't tell. Who would I have told? If I had told Aunt Judith, I would have gotten in trouble for not telling after the first time. And I am sure she would have told me it was my fault. One time, when I was around nine years old, Aunt Judith caught me rubbing my private parts. She told me it was a terrible thing that my sister Haylee had taught me. So, I knew she would never believe me if I told her what was really going on. Everything was always my fault. Why would this be any different?

Each time after he touched me, after he did what he did, I would wash my hands with as much soap as possible. It was never enough. I would scrub my body in the shower but *not* the bath, as I didn't want it to soak into me. It needed to be washed away. I became very aware of the people around me in every situation. A bump into me or a longer-than-normal look in my direction made me squirm, uncomfortable, and self-conscious, like I needed to hide myself. I thought they could see it on me, that I was impure.

That young man took something from me, something I didn't even know I had to give. It had a profound impact on how I related to men then and how I continue to relate to men now.

As I grew older and began to understand the weight of what had happened, the truth of it rearranged everything. He hadn't been spending time with me for my sake. He had been spending time with me for his. The one person who gave me attention, attention I was so desperate for, had been causing me more harm than anyone. And when I finally understood that, I felt abandoned by him too.

CHAPTER EIGHT

THE DRIVE

It was strange, perhaps even eerie, that Aunt Judith's house was so close to the house where I had lived with Mom and Dad. The house where Mom's body was found, buried by the well. At first, I was happy about it because the area was familiar to me, and I had memories there, memories of being with Mom, Dad, Haylee, Brian, and Lisa. But that feeling didn't last. Aunt Judith would always drive by my old house when we were on our way into town. There was another route she could take, but she chose the most traumatic one. Maybe she didn't realize. I don't know. She never asked me how it made me feel, and I don't remember ever telling her. After all, we didn't talk about our feelings. Ever.

I remember staring out the window at that house, my house, Mom and Dad's house, every time we drove by. I wanted to stop there and feel the sense of my family being back together again, as if standing in its presence could somehow undo the past. I imagined that standing in the yard might bring Mom back, might change the final moments of her life, might allow for a do-over.

It made me tearful, driving by that house. I wanted to go inside. I wanted to walk through each room to remember what it felt like to live there. I imagined running through the house from room to room and ending back where I started, just like I used to do. I pictured myself going upstairs, sitting on the beds in the bedroom with Haylee, Brian, and Lisa, and talking like we used to do. I imagined walking into the kitchen, sitting at the table with everyone while we ate dinner, just like before. I wanted to relive every moment in that house.

Most desirably, I wanted to feel wanted again, the way I felt with Mom and Dad.

The memories of Mom and Dad were fading and were few and far between. Nobody talked to me about them, and I was starting to forget. I wanted so badly to remember.

Our house

CHAPTER NINE

FREEDOM DENIED

At some point, Brian and Lisa were also moved from Michigan. I'm foggy about when this happened or where they went to live. I know that a little while after I moved in with Aunt Judith, Lisa came to live there too. I was so extremely happy to have her with me; I instantly felt reassured simply by being near her. Finally, somebody I could relate to and somebody I could talk to who might actually care about me and understand my feelings. She was only there for a couple of weeks, though. One morning, she told me that Uncle Vincent was going to pick her up from school and take her to live with him.

I was initially sad and shocked, then I became elated. I wanted to go live with him too, more than anything, and I told her that. She agreed to tell him to pick me up from school after he got her.

I was so happy at the thought of leaving Aunt Judith's house. I joyously anticipated the sense of being freed from her claws. As I prepared to get on the bus for school that morning, I looked around my bedroom to see if there was anything I needed to take with me that I didn't want to leave behind. Sadly, I didn't have much, so there wasn't much I was attached to. I did pack my crochet hook and yarn; apparently, those things were very important to me. Before I left the bedroom, I stood in the doorway with a smile on my face and gave it one last look, as if I was saying goodbye. Then down the stairs I ran and out to the bus stop I raced.

All day, I waited, constantly checking the door, watching the clock, and paying absolutely no attention to anything the teacher was saying. I had far more important things on my mind than what she was teaching. I daydreamed about the love and acceptance I would be covered with in Uncle Vincent's presence; the time I would spend with the family I hadn't had any contact with; and the stories he could tell me about my mom and dad. I couldn't wait. The anticipation of his arrival was almost too much for me to contain.

The day crept along slowly. The clock ticked from one hour to the next. Uncle Vincent never came.

I couldn't believe it. Why didn't he come to pick me up? Did Lisa forget to tell him about me? Was he just running late? I was confused and angry, and my heart was crushed. I had grown accustomed to people letting me down, and I started to accept the worst, that he wasn't coming. Then I thought maybe he hadn't picked Lisa up that day after all, that when I got off the bus, Lisa would be home at Aunt Judith's with some explanation about why we hadn't been picked up yet.

The 40-minute bus ride home seemed to take hours as I eagerly awaited getting there to see Lisa and to find out what had happened. I walked into the house. I didn't see Lisa. I checked every room. The little bit of hope I was clinging to faded more and more with each empty room. Lisa was nowhere to be found. She was gone. She left me. She and Uncle Vincent had left me behind.

The feelings I had that day were awful. The sadness, the inability to understand why they didn't want me, the realization that my one chance at freedom was gone and that I was stuck in my current situation with no way out. It all took a toll on me, on my psyche, and on how I saw myself in the world in relation to everyone else. It also significantly impacted how I related to others. In my mind, nobody wanted me. I wasn't good enough. There was something wrong with me. I was a problem. That's how I felt, and I heard it almost daily from Aunt Judith, if not through her words, then through her actions. And now, Uncle Vincent didn't want me either? How could that be? I couldn't wrap my head around it. They left me too.

CHAPTER TEN

CALCULATED ISOLATION

One thing I quickly learned while living with Aunt Judith was that I was not allowed to see any of my dad's family. They weren't allowed to visit me, and I wasn't allowed to visit them. I couldn't talk to them on the phone or even write them letters. No contact was permitted. This was agonizing for me. Not only did I love seeing my dad's side of the family, but many of them lived in the neighboring town, literally less than ten minutes away from my new home. It was like I had been transplanted into a whole new existence when I moved into Aunt Judith's house, except I knew they were all still out there. I had been torn from my sister Sophia's house, where I saw my dad's side of the family at least once a week, to suddenly not being allowed to see any of them at all, ever. Talk about confusing. I didn't know what to make of it. Aunt Judith just cut them out of my life, and I had to deal with it alone, of course, and move on.

As an adult, I obtained this letter that was written by Uncle Vincent to Dad:

2)

Haley visited us just that one time. The Kids haven't seen LAURA Louise since June 6th, in Sturgis.

Judith let FRANK Sr. talk to Laura on the phone one time. The second time FRANK called Judith talked nice to FRANK, but hung up when he asked to talk to LAURA Louise. But, THANK God, she's leaving Brian and Lisa Alone.

We are going to Sea-World this weekend.

We went to Italian Day on the last Sunday in July. I brought all of Vincent's Kids. The Kids Rode for 3 hrs on $12.00. Every ride was only 25¢. They had free orange aid, ice cream bars, balloons! - All day!

Jane was excused from being a witness Witness via a Doctor's letter and the District Attorney's kindness and the plea bargaining that's going on.

She was 2 months pregnant, but lost it last Wednesday. The kids and I go to church regularly. Brian is studying to

which showed me that everybody knew that I was being kept away at that time.

I couldn't express any feelings about being kept from them with anybody because they would go unheard, and I would get in trouble for questioning Aunt Judith. As I've said before, I didn't have anybody to talk to. Who around me would even listen, let alone understand, or even try to understand, what I was going through? Aunt Judith wouldn't talk to me about it, probably because she didn't have a good reason, but more accurately because she never felt she had to explain herself to anyone, let alone to someone as *annoying* and *insignificant* as me.

So, there I was again, alone with all these confusing feelings and no idea how to handle them. I'm sure I was a difficult child, a handful, because I likely acted out as a result of everything I was feeling. I truly didn't know how to handle myself, and nobody was helping me process any of it.

Uncle Vincent

I remember one time Uncle Vincent drove by my house while I was outside playing. He stopped his car and said hi to me. To say I was caught off guard is an understatement. I froze. I wanted to talk to him. I wanted to see how he was doing and tell him how I was doing. I wanted to tell him to take me away from this unbearable life in which I was now living. I knew that he cared about me, even though he had previously left me behind, and I desperately wanted to feel that. But instead, I just stood there, frozen in my spot. I didn't even say hello; I didn't say anything. I was too busy contemplating my response to the situation. I didn't know how he would react if I told him what was going on, and I was confident that Aunt Judith would manipulate him into not believing any of what I had to say, and that I would be stuck there in the aftermath. I had to protect myself the only way I knew how. After a few seconds, I ran into the house. I knew I would get in a ton of trouble if she saw me talking to him, so I chose the option that would cause me the least amount of hassle. I'm honestly surprised I didn't get in trouble for him being there at all, as if somehow I might have summoned him. The control Aunt Judith had over me was tremendous.

Michigan Siblings

Another time, my Michigan siblings came to Aunt Judith's house to visit with me. I was overjoyed when I saw them parked out front. As quickly as I could, I raced down the steps to greet them. As I reached the bottom of the stairs, Aunt Judith stopped me. Her face was stone cold. She told me to go back upstairs. My heart stopped. All of the excitement drained from me. What was she talking about? Why would I go back upstairs when they were out front? I told her that they were outside, but of course, she already knew. The look on her face told me that she knew, that she was going to "handle it," and that I wasn't to be a part of it. I couldn't believe it. Aunt Judith really wouldn't let me go outside; she wouldn't let me see them. I stared at her in disbelief. I was overcome with a deep sadness combined with anger and bewildering confusion. This decision made no sense to me. She repeated to me to go back upstairs. I begrudgingly turned around and made my way back up the steps. The internal rage I felt toward Aunt Judith intensified, as did my feelings of loneliness.

When I got to my room, I looked out of my front bedroom window at them. They were gathered on the gravel that made up the front parking area next to the road in front of our house. I was on the second floor of the house, and the porch roof was right on the other side of my window. I thought, *I can easily climb out the window onto that roof; I'd done it before.* I contemplated opening my window and doing just that, of escaping to them. My mind drifted to a daydream of me moving back to Michigan with them. A smile came across my face as I imagined the happiness I would feel. Aunt Judith saw me looking out at them, scolded me for it, and told me I had to close the blinds. I didn't want to, but I didn't have a choice. I took one long, last look outside at all of them, then reluctantly closed the blinds.

Why wouldn't she let me see them? They had never hurt me. They had cared for me, and I longed for them. Plus, they were my siblings. Why wouldn't she ask me how I was feeling about it? What was she afraid of? I walked around my room in circles, trying to figure out a way to escape it. Where could I go? What options did I have? Would my siblings really take me back to Michigan with them? Could I go and live with Uncle Vincent? If I ran away, could I find my way to a better place? I couldn't come up with a solid plan; I didn't know enough to have any real options. I hated living there. I hated my life.

After what felt like hours, Aunt Judith called me downstairs. I knew my siblings were still outside because I had been sneaking peeks out the blinds every now and then. I couldn't even guess why she wanted to see me. With guarded hostility, I walked down the stairs. What did I do wrong this time? Did she see me peeking out the window? Was I being punished for them showing up to see me? Was I going to be required to sit in a windowless room until they left? I didn't know what to expect from her. Then, as calmly as could be, with no explanation, she told me that I could go out onto the front porch to visit with them. *Was this some kind of joke? A test of some sort that I had to pass without knowing the rules? Had I fallen asleep and was in the middle of a dream?* No, it was real. She was actually letting me see them. I couldn't believe she changed her mind. She never changed her mind.

As quickly as I could, I rushed out the front door with as much joy in my heart as it could hold. I hugged each of them so tightly; I didn't want to let go. They embraced me back, and it was so comforting, like coming home. They were so happy to see me; it made my insides jump for joy. I hadn't felt that type of affection since I'd moved to Pennsylvania. They wanted me. They were genuinely concerned about me and had come all this way just to see me. I was important to them.

I wanted to tell them everything I was going through. I wanted to leave with them more than one can imagine, to escape the negative, controlling, abusive environment in which I was stuck. But I held back. I could feel Aunt Judith's eyes on me, like she was watching my every move and making mental notes of any missteps I might make so she could address them with me later. I knew I couldn't say anything. I didn't know who I could trust, and if I told them what was going on and they left me there, there would be hell to pay after they were gone. So, I kept quiet. I didn't tell them anything.

They were probably saddened by my appearance, to be honest. You could literally see the decline in my care just by looking at me. When I was in Michigan, Sophia kept my hair nice and pretty, even in bows. But when I moved to Pennsylvania, I was basically on my own, and my pretty hair was chopped off. I looked completely neglected.

Laura - In Michigan

Laura - In Pennsylvania

The visit seemed to end in the blink of an eye. As I walked back into the house after they left, I could literally feel the happiness I'd just felt with them drain from me, like a chunk of my soul had left with them. I could also feel the weight of the stress, anger, and resentment reclaiming its space within me.

My take on it is that since they had arrived unexpectedly, Aunt Judith was caught off guard, and that's why she initially would not let them see me. I also think she was afraid that they were there to take me away from her, though I don't know why she would've even cared if they did, except that then she would've lost. It likely boils down to the fact that she didn't have control over the situation, so she had to find a way to gain control over it before she would comply with their wishes to see me. I have a feeling that they told her they weren't leaving until they got to see me. I speculate that when she did agree to let them see me, it was with the agreement that they wouldn't contact me again. I say that because I never saw them again after that visit until I was older and sought them out on my own. Either I am correct that such an agreement was made that they wouldn't contact me again, or they left me too.

Brian and Lisa

As for Brian and Lisa, I'm not sure how things progressed, but I know they both ended up living with Grandma, Mom's mom, and Aunt Shirley in Kansas. The only times I got to see them were the times Aunt Judith loaded us all up in the van and drove us across the country to Kansas. If memory serves me correctly, this happened every few years.

Two full days of driving across the country, filled with laughing together, arguing about random inconveniences, and singing along to Hank Williams Jr. cassette tapes. We would leave early in the morning and stop to sleep at bedtime, then we would start back on the road early in the next morning and would drive until we arrived around supper time. It was a long boring drive, but well worth it because once we arrived, I got to see Brian and Lisa.

That was the highlight of every trip to Kansas for me. I loved seeing them.

They lived in a small A-frame house with Grandma. Aunt Shirley lived in a trailer next door, separated by only a driveway. I remember spending time at both houses, soaking up as much time as I could with Brian and Lisa. I remember taking (supervised) walks around the property with them to see their rabbits and chickens, and I remember playing board games with them. I don't remember much else. We were never really left alone together; I think the adults didn't want us talking about all the secrets they were keeping from us.

We'd stay for about a week, then suddenly, without notice, we would be told to get in the van; that it was time to go. These visits typically ended abruptly because Aunt Judith and Grandma would get into an argument. That's how I remember it anyway.

After moving to Aunt Judith's, those trips were the only contact I had with Brian and Lisa. I don't even remember writing letters to them or receiving letters from them. Also, Grandma must've been keeping Brian and Lisa from Dad's family too, because this letter was sent to her from Uncle Vincent's attorney:

Joseph V. Bullano
Attorney & Counselor at Law

COPY

Law Offices
SUITE 462 FIRST NATIONAL BANK BLDG.
New Castle, Pennsylvania 16101

AREA CODE 412 658-1648

August 31, 1982

Mrs.

Portersville, PA 16051

        Re: Request for Visitation Rights
             Minor Children: . Iannarelli and
                                    Iannarelli

Dear Mrs.   :.

Please be advised that I represent Mr.   nnarelli who has
consulted with me relative obtaining visitation rights to the above
referenced minor children of his brother, who are in your custody
and control.

This letter is not to be construed in any way as one that would
cause harrassment or legal dispute concerning the custody of the
two minor children, but it is intended to produce some communication
that would result in an open and liberal visitation relationship by
and between the children and their uncle. This request is specifically proposed in the best interest and welfare of the children to
enable my client to perform the responsibilities expected of their
father's brother under the regrettable circumstances of which we
are all aware. Moreover, it is respectfully suggested that you hold
no animosity toward my client for the actions of his brother and not
deprive the children of what their uncle can do for them at a most
critical time in their lives.

Without the necessity of noting all the reasons why an open and liberal visitation policy should exist in this regard, I appeal to your
sense of fairness and request that you contact my office either
directly, or through an attorney, so that arrangements may be under-
taken to create a spirit of cooperation which will inure to the
benefit and best interest of the children who are of primary concern
in this regard.

Your cooperation is most sincerely appreciated.

                        Respectfully yours,

                        Joseph V. Bullano

JVB:lam

Haylee

Once in a blue moon, Aunt Judith would take me to visit Aunt Martha, another one of Mom's sisters. That's when I found out where Haylee was. She had been there the whole time. I was thrilled to see my sister! I couldn't contain my excitement!

Haylee had a boyfriend, Robert, who was always nice to me. They even took me on a date with them once, to the movies, I think. It was so much fun.

I remember another time, after Haylee and Robert got married, they visited with me at Aunt Judith's house. We went for a walk to the ice cream stand, and Robert carried me back on his shoulders. I felt like a million bucks!

Those are the only times I remember seeing Haylee while I lived with Aunt Judith, until I was older and visited her on my own. As an adult, I found out Haylee had visited Dad in prison. She said she was in his room and that he was chained to his bed. I couldn't understand why the visit would take place in his jail cell, but I hadn't been there, so I didn't know.

Recently, I learned she had actually visited him on two occasions: once in prison and once in the hospital. That made more sense; he was chained to his hospital bed. Oh, how I wish she had taken me with her, but she didn't. I think Haylee must have been afraid of Aunt Judith too.

I guess you could say that I lost all of my siblings in the process of moving in with Aunt Judith. I wasn't allowed to talk to them on the phone or anything. I only got to see them on the few occasions I mentioned above. Chalk up more losses for me to deal with - alone.

CHAPTER ELEVEN

THE DISTANT EMBRACE

Memories around this time I speak of are all fuzzy, although I remember an event that I believe happened when I was in fourth grade. I am sure I wasn't in third grade because I started at Mohawk Elementary in third grade, where I had a classroom downstairs with a female teacher, and the memory I am referring to wasn't in that classroom, and my teacher was a man. However, I do remember a few things that happened in third grade.

I remember that I had a friend at my table, and we must have been causing trouble together because one day we put each other's names on our papers as a joke and turned them in. Nobody ever knew. I also remember how my third-grade classroom was arranged. My desk was in a cluster of four along the coat wall next to the teacher's desk, where I was positioned to face the front of the room. The door to the room was at the back of the classroom. I remember that because I had a habit of turning around to look at the doorway, hoping my mom would come to pick me up. I imagined this was all just a bad dream, a misunderstanding, that she wasn't really gone, and that at any moment she would walk into the room and take me home.

I don't think the memory I'm referring to happened in fifth grade either because our elementary school moved to a new building then, and this event took place in the old building. So, I'm pretty sure it was fourth grade.

So, there I was, sitting in my fourth-grade classroom when the guidance counselor appeared at the door and asked me to step into the hallway. I figured I was in trouble for something again, but I went, reluctantly.

He handed me a letter. It was from my dad, from prison. I couldn't believe it. I hadn't had any contact with him since Mom died, except maybe one or two phone calls with him while I lived in Michigan. Nobody had even mentioned his name around me.

I held the letter, staring at it, unsure of what to say or whether or not I should open it. I remember thinking it wasn't even strange that the letter came to the school. Surely by then Dad knew that I was living with Aunt Judith, and he knew that she wouldn't give it to me if he had sent it to the house.

As I stood there holding the letter, my heart was pounding. I was filled with a mix of nervousness and excitement. I was happy to hear from him, but I also felt sick thinking about what he had done to Mom, and thus indirectly to me. How could I open it? But how could I not? I wanted to know what he had to say. So, I read the letter.

Today, I couldn't tell you what that letter said; it was so long ago. I wish I still had it, but I don't. All I can say is that knowing that he was trying to get in touch with me made me feel warm inside, like he hadn't forgotten about me as it seemed everyone else had. It felt like a piece of my old life was checking in on me, and for a moment, I felt solace.

That feeling, though, was short-lived because I knew I was going to get in trouble for receiving the letter when I got home. I was definitely going to be in trouble for opening it. Aunt Judith would be mad and blame me for it. Like I said before, everything was always my fault with her. I thought about not telling her about it at all, but Dad had sent me $5. I think it was around my birthday because I seem to remember the $5 being a birthday gift. So, if I didn't tell her where it came from, she would have accused me of stealing it.

When I got home, I reluctantly showed her the letter. As expected, she was furious, and I got in trouble not for receiving it, but for opening it. She angrily took it from me. I have no idea where that letter went; I never saw it again. I was glad I opened it and read it, though. If I hadn't, she would have taken it, like she did, and then I never would have gotten to read it at all. It was worth getting in trouble for, reading Dad's words.

She must have called the school and told them not to allow it to happen again, though, because I never got another letter.

CHAPTER TWELVE

THE STRUGGLE TO BELONG

They say that experiencing trauma as a child, whether it be violence, the loss of a parent, sexual abuse, or other traumatic events, has a strong correlation with low self-esteem. I had experienced all of these. Trauma, if not properly addressed, which of course in my case it was not, can cause the child to develop a warped sense of self-worth and foster deep internalized feelings of being bad or unlovable.

Top that off with living in an environment that shows no acceptance or affection and lacks guidance and understanding. I was doomed.

Before I moved in with Aunt Judith, I had friends wherever I went. Each time we moved to a new place, I made friends instantly. I was comfortable with myself, confident even. This was before I was made to question everything about myself. So now, making friends no longer came naturally to me. I think I tried too hard because I had such low self-esteem, so in my efforts to make friends, I actually pushed them away. I approached each situation believing that nobody wanted to be around me, that I wasn't good enough. I tried really hard to get them to change their minds, even though I had subconsciously created the struggle in my own mind to begin with.

I didn't have guidance on how to be a friend, so even if I managed to make friends, I quickly became annoying to them, and they wouldn't want to continue being around me. I was my own worst enemy.

Amy, Heather, and I had neighbors all around us. This made it a little easier to have someone to play with anyway. There was a group of us that would hang out together pretty regularly. Aunt Judith's daughter Debbie got married and moved a couple of miles down the road. She would let us come down to her house pretty much whenever we wanted to. Sometimes we would walk there; sometimes we would ride our bikes. I loved the freedom of being allowed to ride my bike on the road.

We had friends at Debbie's house too. It just so happened that the friends across the street from her house were related to some of the friends from our neighborhood. We spent a lot of time with all of these friends. We rode our bikes together, had sleepovers, smoked cigarettes (I started smoking at age 12), and built cabins. We built some of the best cabins together. I had great times with them. Internally, though, I never felt like I fit in. I always felt like I was trying to convince them of my worth. If they "picked me" for the day, I was overjoyed, but if they didn't, I felt left out, alone, and devastated. There was no happy medium for me. I took it as rejection.

I think the problem was that I felt so unwanted at home that I needed the steadiness of being consistently chosen somewhere, so I sought it in friendships. I wanted them to be my friends all the time, and if we had the slightest disagreement or if they wanted to play with someone else, I took it extremely personally and immediately thought I did something wrong. Furthermore, when that did happen, I expected them to never want to be around me again, so I had to convince them again. This unhealthy and unproductive cycle repeated throughout my childhood and even somewhat into adulthood.

At school, the feelings of being alone were louder, heavier, and even more evident than at home. Every day, I would get off the bus and walk into the school alone. As I walked to my locker, I would notice the other students. It seemed that all around me were groups of friends laughing, talking, and enjoying each other's company.

Some were standing together along the wall watching others walk by; others were walking together in groups. Every now and then I would see someone running up to greet their friend who had just arrived. I felt envious of them, of all of them. I would continue on my way and put my stuff into my locker. Then I would look around and try to decide what to do next because I didn't have a friend in particular I was looking for, and nobody was looking for me. The loneliness of it made me so sad inside, and it fed my belief that I was unlikable, even unlovable. Why didn't anybody see me that way? Why wasn't anybody running down the hall to greet me? *What was wrong with me?*

Amy and I were in the same grade. She had a lot of school friends. Amy would try to include me in things, which I appreciated. Some of the kids were nice to me, but I continued to always feel like they didn't truly like me, like I wasn't good enough.

In sixth grade, our school went to camp for three days. I didn't have any close friends, so even though I was excited to go to camp and to be away from Aunt Judith, I dreaded it at the same time. I was put in a cabin with four other girls. They were all friends with each other, and then there was me. They all snuck out of the cabin one night to go and see the boys, but I wasn't invited to go along. Instead, they gave me their candy stash and told me I could eat whatever I wanted since I wasn't going with them.

So, I stayed in the cabin by myself. I acted like it wasn't a big deal as they left, but I was crumbling inside. Once I knew they were gone, I cried and cried. I stared at the big empty room, studying the carvings in the wood left by previous campers. I asked God why this was my life. Why me? What was wrong with me?

I felt so alone. I couldn't understand why nobody wanted to be my friend. Slowly, I sifted through the pity candy they had left for me. I don't know if I actually ate any of it or not.

At the time, I told myself maybe I was imagining it. Maybe it wasn't as bad as I thought. But deep down, I knew the truth. And years later, when I was an adult, I got proof. I was having a conversation with one of the girls who had been in that cabin. She casually mentioned how they had been made to room with someone they didn't like and how mad they were about it. She even said the girl's name, a different girl, but I knew it wasn't really the girl she had mentioned. It was me.

Her words hit me like a ton of bricks. All those years ago I had wondered if I had overreacted, if maybe I had misunderstood the situation. But no, I had been right. They really didn't want me there. The sadness of that realization took me straight back to sixth grade, to that empty room, to the carvings in the wood, to the unanswered questions I had cried into the darkness.

It's funny how I thought I had healed from it, that I had moved on. But in that moment, all those feelings of being unwanted, alone, and not good enough came rushing back.

I never told her that it was really me.

One time I wanted my hair cut like my neighbor Lisa's. She had a short pixie cut. Lisa was a year older than I was. She had a lot of friends, and I thought if I had my hair like hers somehow that would make me have a lot of friends too. I was so excited when my aunt told me I could have the same haircut. I enthusiastically went to a family member's home, who I think was training to become a beautician, so she could transform my hair, my life. I sat there for what seemed like hours getting my hair fixed up. I was as patient as I had ever been. Finally, it was time to take a look.

The exhilaration vanished the moment I saw my reflection. As I stared into the mirror, all of the excitement drained from me. This wasn't what I had asked for. It looked nothing like Lisa's. Instead, I was now the unfortunate owner of a full head of permed hair.

I retreated to a room by myself and cried. How could this mistake have been made? Why was my hair permed? When I told Aunt Judith this wasn't what I wanted, she simply shrugged her shoulders and said, "Oh well," as if it was no big deal, as if my wants were as insignificant as I was, as if nothing I thought or felt ever really mattered. Aunt Judith knew I was getting a perm the whole time and not a pixie cut. She had lied to me.

I was furious with her. Hurt by her. Again. And now, I was embarrassed for anyone to see me with this awful hairstyle. Once again, I was reminded that I couldn't trust Aunt Judith.

So much for my plan to win friends with a new haircut.

The years went on. I remember sitting in high school, I was probably in eighth grade, hating my life, staring at the clock as the seconds crept by. Feeling all alone, like I had nobody. I wished I could switch schools. I thought that if I could just start over in a school where nobody knew me, I would be able to form friendships. Of course, that wasn't an option.

CHAPTER THIRTEEN

CONTINUED DECEPTION

NEW CASTLE NEWS, SATURDAY, JUNE 20, 1981

TWO

DA gets extra time for Iannarelli trial

The district attorney received extra time yesterday for trying murder suspect Frank C. Iannarelli.

Judge William R. Balph extended the time under Rule 1100 of state criminal procedure. He extended it until next Friday, the last day of this month's session of criminal trials. It was at least the second extension granted in the case.

Rule 1100 requires that trials for criminal defendants start within 180 days of arrest or the defendant can possibly go free without trial.

Judges can extend the 180-day limit if they rule the prosecution asked for an extension before the deadline expired and it tried diligently to bring the case to trial.

Iannarelli, 53, of Union Valley Road, Shenango Township, faces charges of first and second degree murder in the death of his wife, Laura Lee Iannarelli, 33. They were separated at the time of her death.

Her body was found buried in a shallow grave Aug. 11, 1980, beside Iannarelli's residence. She was last seen alive at 6 a.m. that day.

Cause of death was multiple gunshot wounds in the chest.

State police arrested Iannarelli that night.

Court-appointed defense attorneys Dominick Motto and Norman Barilla had requested that charges against Iannarelli be dismissed under Rule 1100.

District Attorney Donald E. Williams had requested the time for trial be extended.

Balph held a brief hearing yesterday morning before he extended the time.

A major part of the hearing centered on whether or not Williams had requested the extension soon enough. He had to request it by May 1.

Williams stated that his request bore the date April 29 and the stamp of President Judge Glenn McCracken. The request was formally filed May 8.

Motto questioned whether or not McCracken or his secretary, Mickey Pagley, had stamped the request and charged that if Miss Pagley made the stamp, April 29 would not count as the date of filing. May 8, a week after the deadline, would be the date of filing in that case, he argued.

Williams called Miss Pagley to the stand and she testified that she did not make the stamp. She reported the stamp belonged to McCracken and no one else normally used it.

The other issue discussed yesterday involved the time needed for Iannarelli's mental examination at Farview State Hospital.

Defense attorneys had given notice March 26 of plans to use an insanity defense.

About two weeks later, Williams requested a mental examination of Iannarelli his competence to stand trial. Iannarelli was returned to Lawrence County last Monday.

Motto argued that Iannarelli's stay at Farview should be counted against the commonwealth because it sent him there.

Williams replied that the time should not count against the commonwealth because the defendant was unavailable for trial.

Balph ruled that the issue was irrelevant at the present time, but could become relevant if more extensions were requested.

Monday, June 22, 1[...]

Iannarelli enters plea of guilty

Frank C. Iannarelli, 53, of Union Valley Road, Shenango Township, pleaded guilty this morning before Judge William R. Balph in Lawrence County court.

Iannarelli is facing charges of first and second degree murder for killing his wife, Laura Lee Iannarelli, 33, on Aug. 12, 1980.

Balph will preside over a degree of guilt hearing, the time and date of which will be announced.

If he is found guilty of first degree murder, Iannarelli has the right to withraw his plea. If, in the plea bargaining, he is found guilty of third degree murder, the Commonwealth will recommend a sentence of five to 15 years imprisonment.

The body of Mrs. Iannarelli was found buried in a shallow grave Aug. 12, next to Iannarelli's residence. She was last seen alive at 8 a.m. that day. Cause of death was determined as multiple gunshot wounds of the chest. State police arrested Iannarelli that night. The couple was separated at the time.

Iannarelli's guilty plea was entered, following Balph's granting the district attorney a trial extension. The extension was granted after a brief hearing Friday.

Balph extended the time until Friday this week under Rule 1100 of state criminal procedure. Friday is the last day of this month's session of criminal

Iannarelli degree of guilt hearing set

By DON NAKLES
News Staff Writer

The degree of guilt hearing for Frank C. Iannarelli, who pleaded guilty to charges he shot his estranged wife, will begin on July 16.

Iannarelli, 53, of Union Valley Road, Shenango Township, pleaded guilty yesterday morning to a general charge of murder before Judge William R. Balph.

Iannarelli is charged with first and third degree murder arising from the Aug. 12 shooting of Laura Lee Iannarelli. Her body was found buried in a shallow grave next to his residence. She died of multiple gunshot wounds to the chest.

Iannarelli's plea "supports murder in the third degree," Balph stated.

First degree murder differs from third degree in that it requires at least brief premeditation, Balph said.

Dominick Motto, appointed as co-defense counsel in October, said that he believed the plea bargain to be a finding of third degree after which the district attorney would recommend a sentence of from five to 15 years imprisonment.

District Attorney Donald E. Williams stated he believed the plea bargain to be that he would recommend that sentence only if Balph found third degree. He said he was leaving the decision on degree of guilt to Balph.

Williams agreed that the defendant could withdraw his plea if Balph found him guilty of first degree.

Balph will rule after a degree of guilt hearing. The evidence and witnesses presented at the hearing would resemble a jury trial without a jury, Balph stated.

Balph will preside over the hearing in which the prosecution may try proving Iannarelli guilty of first degree. Williams declined to promise he would not try proving first degree murder.

Williams reported the commonwealth has evidence that Iannarelli committed first degree murder and that he expected the defense to present evidence in Iannarelli's favor.

The defense may attempt proving the defendant is guilty of a lesser charge, voluntary manslaughter.

In light of the upcoming hearing, Balph declined to ask Iannarelli for his version of the incident as usual before accepting or rejecting a plea bargain. He did ask Williams to give the prosecution's version of the incident.

According to Williams, Iannarelli was living on Union Valley Road with his three children and Mrs. Iannarelli was living with another man, _______ in Pertersville on Aug. 12.

Iannarelli and his wife jointly owned the Union Valley Road house and Mrs. Iannarelli went there to arrange for the house's sale.

_______ learned from Mrs. Iannarelli's employer that she had not reported for work.

He went to the Iannarelli home and Iannarelli told him Mrs. Iannarelli left around 11 a.m. _______ found Mrs. Iannarelli's vehicle abandoned near the home and returned to the house.

In the yard, he spotted a patch of freshly-dug dirt and found a foot a few inches underground. He called police from a neighbor's house and the police and Iannarelli arrived simultaneously.

Investigators found a gun in Iannarelli's kitchen which ballistic tests later proved to be the gun that fired three shots into Mrs. Iannarelli, Williams reported.

Iannarelli admitted to police "that this was his wife and he had shot her," according to Williams.

"Yes, I made that statement to the state police but at that time I did not know it was my wife lying out there," the defendant said. "I was told that ballistics reports showed it was my pistol."

Iannarelli replied that he was unaware of parts of Williams' version and added that he believed he shot her although he did not remember the specific act.

Suspect says he can't remember shooting wife

By DON NAKLES
News Staff Writer

Frank C. Iannarelli testified for about two hours in his own defense yesterday and said he did not remember firing the gunshots that killed his wife.

Iannarelli, 53, of Union Valley Road, Shenango Township, testified in the second day of his degree of guilt hearing at the Lawrence County Government Center. The hearing was to resume this morning.

He pleaded guilty on June 22 to a general charge of criminal homicide. He had faced first and third degree murder charges for killing his wife, Laura Lee Iannarelli, 33. Her body was found on Aug. 12, 1980 in a shallow grave.

Judge William R. Balph will determine the degree of Iannarelli's guilt through evidence presented at the hearings which resemble a trial with no jury.

IANNARELLI'S plea bargain allows him to withdraw his guilty plea if Balph finds him guilty of first degree.

District Attorney Donald E. Williams has agreed, also as part of the plea bargain, to recommend a sentence of five to 15 years imprisonment if Balph finds Iannarelli guilty of third degree.

On the stand, Iannarelli described marital problems that began in 1975 and climaxed in the shooting on his birthday.

The problems included his attempts, sometimes unsuccessful, to see the couple's four children, now aged 9 to 16, while his wife had custody of them.

The marriage improved until early 1977. Mrs. Iannarelli bought her aunt's restaurant in Bessemer and Iannarelli co-signed an $8,000 mortgage on the couple's house.

Mrs. Iannarelli promised to work elsewhere to pay back the loan if the restaurant failed, Iannarelli recalled.

In 1978, the restaurant failed because of unpaid bills, Iannarelli revealed, although Mrs. Iannarelli had said the restaurant was doing well. Shortly after the closure, Iannarelli "gave her hell" for lying about the restaurant.

THE NEXT morning, she said she was going to drive the children in the family truck to the restaurant, Iannarelli testified, but he did not see her or the children "for a full five months."

"I did not know where she or anybody was," Iannarelli added. Iannarelli quit making payments on the truck's $2,000 loan so the bank stepped in and found Mrs. Iannarelli in Grand Bay, Ala.

Iannarelli suspected his wife had sold the truck since she did not need a title to sell it in Alabama and his insurance company refused to pay his claim on the truck.

Mrs. Iannarelli told the bank the truck broke down and was stolen, according to Iannarelli, but he tried unsuccessfully to find her in Grand Bay.

A few days later, Mrs. Iannarelli phoned and invited him to spend

See IANNARELLI, page 5

Iannarelli From page 2

Thanksgiving in Grand Bay. "She talked like she wanted to come back," he recalled.

HE RETURNED home after Thanksgiving and next saw them at Christmas, 1978 when his wife and children came here. Two days after Christmas, Mrs. Iannarelli returned to Alabama but left the children with Iannarelli.

On New Year's Eve Mrs. Iannarelli's sister forcibly took the children to Alabama, Iannarelli alleged.

He saw the children next in the summer of 1979 shortly after his _______ daughter _______ phoned him. At Mrs. Iannarelli's Alabama residence, Iannarelli found three of his children.

Wiping tears from his eyes, Iannarelli continued that one of his other two daughters asked if they could return to Pennsylvania with him. He then drove them here.

_______ returned here later but an aunt took two of the children back to Alabama.

He saw the other two children next in the summer of 1980 after Mrs. Iannarelli and the children returned here. One of the two children staying with Iannarelli then returned to live with Mrs. Iannarelli, according to his testimony.

CRYING, IANNARELLI testified that soon he got a letter from one of his daughters that said she felt "like the world's coming to an end" and he got a note from Mrs. Iannarelli's sister that said the three children were "not being treated right."

Soon, with Iannarelli's Aug. 12 birthday approaching, he and his wife agreed that the children could spend his birthday at his house.

The morning of Aug. 12, Iannarelli took the children to a relative's house so that he could shop later for birthday party trimmings. Before leaving the house to shop, Mrs. Iannarelli arrived, he said.

An argument ensued at first over the children, then over a $188 bill for long distance phone calls that she had charged to him. "She said she can make all the phone calls she wants," Iannarelli continued, " . . . and Frank you pay the bill."

They also argued about the truck, the mortgage and her running to relatives' homes. "She was really upset," Iannarelli testified, and she "hit me across the head with" a frying pan.

"I HAD never seen her that vicious before," Iannarelli added, and because of a previous incident he feared her.

He got a pistol from the bedroom to scare her, Iannarelli claimed, but he found her in the kitchen talking through gritted teeth. "You could see a little foam" at her mouth, he said.

Mrs. Iannarelli then said-he would never see their daughters again and, "The girls do as I tell them or I beat them. I am the boss," Iannarelli recalled.

On hearing the word "boss" Iannarelli heard two noises and remembered no more. The next thing he remembered was sitting on his back stoop. "I had a headache," he continued. "I just couldn't realize what I was doing there."

THEN HE noticed the shallow grave with Mrs. Iannarelli's feet sticking out of it. He found no pulse on her body and covered her feet. He said he was about to dial the phone for police when he heard a voice say, "Don't do it Frank 'cause they'll never believe ya."

After the shooting and arrest, Iannarelli underwent a psychiatric examination. A report of it was admitted into evidence yesterday.

"When we consider Mr. Iannarelli's history of chronic, severe marital discord; physical punishment; . . . separation from his children and the fact that he was alone on his birthday . . . it seems possible that the stage may have been set for a catastrophic event," the report concludes.

NEW CASTLE NEWS, SATURDAY, AUGUST 8, 1981

Testimony ends for Iannarelli's guilt hearing

By DON NAKLES
News Staff Writer

Testimony ended yesterday in the degree of guilt hearing for Frank C. Iannarelli, leaving only the attorneys' closing arguments and legal briefs for early next month.

Iannarelli, 53, of Union Valley Road, Shenango Township, pleaded guilty on June 22 to a general charge of criminal homicide. He had faced charges of first and third degree murder for killing his wife, Laura Lee Iannarelli. Her body was found in a shallow grave beside Iannarelli's home last Aug. 12.

Judge William R. Balph will determine the degree of Iannarelli's guilt through evidence presented at the hearings.

A plea bargain allows Iannarelli to withdraw his guilty plea if Balph finds him guilty in the first degree, and District Attorney Donald E. Williams has agreed to recommend a sentence of five to 15 years imprisonment if Balph finds Iannarelli guilty in the third degree.

YESTERDAY'S hearing had been set to begin at 11 a.m. but did not because court-appointed defense attorney Dominick Motto was not notified of the starting time. Motto could not be reached in the morning to be told of the hearing.

Iannarelli's other court-appointed attorney, Norman J. Barilla, was told of the starting time around 11 a.m.

The hearing was rescheduled for 2:30 p.m., but started shortly after then because a juvenile hearing before Balph ran late.

Motto finished his questioning of Iannarelli in the first 15 minutes or so of yesterday's hearing. The defense presented no other witnesses.

Williams then cross-examined Iannarelli for a little more than an hour. Most of Iannarelli's answers matched those he had given yesterday to Motto.

For example, on both days he said he did not remember actually pulling the trigger of his gun, and that he shouted in an argument with his wife just before the shooting and got his gun out in an attempt to scare her.

Iannarelli, however, went into further detail on some matters. He stated that several hours after the shooting he returned to the Union Valley Road residence and found Mrs. Iannarelli's boyfriend there and that he watched as police arrived at the scene.

"I COULDN'T understand what everybody was doing there," Iannarelli testified. "I was all confused."

The boyfriend began shouting at Iannarelli and police handcuffed Iannarelli and put him in a police car. In the car, State Trooper Rodney Fowler asked Iannarelli if he had shot "her."

Iannarelli said he asked who "her" was.

Williams questioned Iannarelli closely on his claim he did not know to whom Fowler was referring and also on his contention that he did not remember the actual shooting.

Williams asked more questions about Iannarelli's failure to return the couple's four children to Mrs. Iannarelli's residence the afternoon of the shooting.

If he did not know he had shot Mrs. Iannarelli, Williams asked, why did he not return the children as agreed.

Iannarelli replied that he knew Mrs. Iannarelli was not home since her boyfriend had come looking for her about 4:30 p.m. The shooting occurred about 10 a.m.

MRS. IANNARELLI had arrived at the Union Valley home between 9:30 and 10 a.m., Iannarelli said, and he noticed "she was disturbed before she got there."

Soon after her arrival, an argument ensued inside the house. Iannarelli stated that he and his wife were shouting, but that only he was making accusations about past incidents. The incidents included the loss of the couple's truck and the failure of their restaurant.

During the argument, Iannarelli alleged that "she moved those kids around like they were cattle," referring to her frequent changes of residence.

Mrs. Iannarelli then struck Iannarelli in the head with a frying pan and Iannarelli got his gun from the bedroom. Iannarelli testified he had bought the gun "to let the whole world know that, well, Frank has a gun now."

The gun apparently failed to scare Mrs. Iannarelli, he said, and force her to converse normally.

"At the point of a gun, is that normal?" Williams asked.

Iannarelli replied that he did not know how to answer that question. He stuck to that answer during Williams' repeated questioning of how he could fail to know, given the circumstances.

Shortly after the shooting, Iannarelli began dialing for police. "I was going to tell police that there was a body lying out there," Iannarelli revealed, but a voice stopped him.

HE LOOKED for the source of the voice but found none. He testified that he had heard the voice before, while lying in bed alone one night.

Iannarelli did not call police because the voice told him no one would believe that a body was outside and he did not know how it got there.

"Do you believe it's any easier to believe now?" Williams asked, and Iannarelli replied that he did not know.

After almost dialing police, Iannarelli drove Mrs. Iannarelli's van from the yard to about a mile down the road and left it. "All that crossed my mind was I'd better move her van from here," Iannarelli answered.

Williams had asked if he moved the van because he could not tell police the van was sitting there with no driver.

Next, Iannarelli said he got a beer. "Having another beer was just automatic with me," he said. "I did drink a lot.

"I would like to know for sure if I shot her," Iannarelli stated. "I would like to know how I carried her outside and why I buried her there."

He continued that he could not have lifted her body in his arms but, upon close questioning by Williams, admitted he could have dragged her body and put it in the shallow grave.

Prosecution completes case against suspect of homicide

By DON NAKLES
News Staff Writer

The prosecution completed its case against homicide suspect Frank C. Iannarelli at a degree of guilty hearing yesterday.

District Attorney Donald E. Williams presented 10 witnesses in the courtroom of Judge William R. Balph and rested his case. The hearing was set to resume today at 1 p.m. with the first defense witness.

Iannarelli, 53, of Union Valley Road, Shenango Township, pleaded guilty on June 22 to a general charge of criminal homicide.

He had faced first and second degree murder charges for killing his wife, Laura Lee Iannarelli, 33, on Aug. 12, 1980. Her body was found in a shallow grave.

BALPH WILL determine the degree of Iannarelli's guilt through evidence presented at hearings. The hearings resemble a trial without a jury present.

The plea bargain allows Iannarelli to withdraw his plea if Balph finds him guilty of first degree.

Williams has agreed, also as part of the plea bargain, to recommend a sentence of five to 15 years imprisonment if Balph finds Iannarelli guilty of third degree. The maximum prison term for a third degree conviction is 10 to 20 years.

One of the commonwealth's chief witnesses, Rodney Fowler of the New Castle State Police, testified that he talked briefly with Iannarelli in a police car parked at the crime scene.

"He (Iannarelli) was talking low," Fowler, the chief investigator of the case, said. "He was nervous, he kept rubbing his hands together.

"I ASKED HIM if he killed his wife," Fowler continued. "He said, 'If you want to know the truth, yes.' I asked, 'How did you do it?' and he said, 'I shot her.'"

Iannarelli showed no emotion or remorse, according to Fowler, and said he shot Mrs. Iannarelli with a .22-callliber gun that was still in the house.

Fowler had only one other conversation with Iannarelli and that occurred three days later in the Lawrence County Jail. There, according to Fowler, Iannarelli told him that he had shot his wife at 10 a.m. that day in the kitchen.

According to Fowler, Iannarelli made no request for an attorney to be present during the conversation in jail.

Police first became involved when Mrs. Iannarelli's boyfriend, ______ ______ of Portersville, took John Hart, Shenango Township police officer, to the grave in Iannarelli's back yard, Hart testified.

HART NOTICED plywood and tires stacked on an area of freshly-dug dirt. He removed the plywood and tires and dug down about six inches. There he found Mrs. Iannarelli's body.

______ was at the scene and began shouting hysterically at Iannarelli, according to Hart. ______ accused Iannarelli of killing Mrs. Iannarelli and Iannarelli insisted he knew nothing about it, Hart and another Shenango Township officer, Richard L. Schweinsberg, testified.

Hart and Schweinsberg took ______ and Iannarelli to separate cars so that they could not reach each other. Hart said he noticed a strong odor of alcohol on Iannarelli's breath.

Shortly thereafter, state police arrested Iannarelli, Schweinsberg said, and took him to the state police station.

There, Iannarelli asked for an attorney and police read him his rights again, according to Schweinsberg.

Schweinsberg knew Iannarelli as his neighbor before the incident and testified Iannarelli had asked his help several times in locating Iannarelli's children.

At the state police station, Iannarelli recognized Schweinsberg as his neighbor and told him Mrs. Iannarelli wanted the house to be sold and the money split.

AFTER FINDING the state police and city police breathalyzers were not working, Schweinsberg took Iannarelli to the hospital for a blood alcohol test. "He (Iannarelli) seemed very calm," Schweinsberg said.

The policeman recalled smelling alcohol on Iannarelli's breath but "there was no stagger in his voice or slur in his voice." Iannarelli "did not appear to be extremely nervous," he said.

Iannarelli also told Schweinsberg that he had called his wife that morning and told her he had a buyer for the house and needed her signature.

Iannarelli said "he had just had all of her he could take," Schweinsberg recalled.

On cross-examination by court-appointed defense attorney Dominick Motto, Schweinsberg reported that he knew before the incident that the Iannarellis were having marital problems and that Iannarelli was unhappy about how often he saw his children.

"He (Iannarelli) stated that he would never sell the house," Schweinsberg said.

SCHWEINSBERG said he had been called to a domestic dispute at the Iannarelli home some months before. Fowler testified he found the residence "cluttered" with dishes, an overflowing garbage can and beer cans in the yard.

While Fowler investigated the house, Dr. William Gillespy, laboratory director for St. Francis Hospital and a pathologist, investigated the cause of death.

He found three small-caliber bullet wounds in Mrs. Iannarelli's body. All three bullets traveled through the body and stopped just under the skin of the back, he testified.

He also found minor, recent bruises on the elbow, thighs, right lower leg and left knee. Powder burns from a gunshot were found on the right upper chest, neck and right cheek, Gillespy said.

Any of the three wounds alone could have killed Mrs. Iannarelli, Gillespy added, and she lived for no more than five minutes after the three quick shots.

One bullet pierced the heart and lung, a second punctured a major vein of the heart area and a lung and a third struck a lung, according to Gillespy.

______, a neighbor, testified that he sold a .22-caliber handgun to Iannarelli about three months before the shooting.

HE RECALLED that Iannarelli had wanted the gun to protect his children. Iannarelli feared that a stranger was watching his house and waiting for a chance to harm the children, according to ______.

Others who testified were city engineer David Kite, State Police Cpl. Richard Baldo, State Police Criminalist Scott Ermlick, State Trooper Paul K. Montag and ______.

Kite identified drawings of the Iannarelli property, Baldo identified 37 photos taken of the crime scene, Ermlick described blood on kitchen furniture, kitchen floor tile and other objects as matching Mrs. Iannarelli's and Montag said he tried unsuccessfully to contact Iannarelli's attorney while at the state police station.

______ testified that Iannarelli invited him over for a beer the afternoon of the murder and saw Iannarelli later at a bar.

"You couldn't tell on Frank," ______ answered when asked if Iannarelli was drunk at the bar. "He could hold his beer pretty well."

______ son ______ had called ______ over to the Iannarelli house after finding something wrong there.

______ testified that ______ and another man came to his house. "One was pretty well shook up and that's why I called the police," the younger ______ said.

COMMONWEALTH OF PENNSYLVANIA) IN THE COURT OF COMMON PLEAS OF
VS.)
) LAWRENCE COUNTY, PENNSYLVANIA
)
FRANK CHARLES IANNARELLI) CRIMINAL DIVISION
)
) NO. 451 of 1980, Cr.

<u>VERDICT</u>

AND NOW, November 25, 1981, following full and complete hearing as to the degree of guilt of the Defendant in the captioned homicide case, the Court hereby finds the Defendant guilty of murder in the third degree and directs that the District Attorney schedule the Defendant for sentencing as of course.

BY THE COURT

_______________________ J.

(MAE)

Iannarelli sentenced for murder

Frank Charles Iannarelli was sentenced yesterday to serve 5 to 15 years at Western Penitentiary of Pittsburgh for the murder of his wife on Aug. 12, 1980.

He will be given credit for 497 days already served and could be eligible to seek parole in about a year.

On June 22 Iannarelli, 54, of Wampum RD 1 pleaded guilty to a general charge of murder. He was found guilty of third degree murder by Judge William R. Balph on Nov. 23.

Iannarelli was charged with first and third degree murder after the body of his wife Laura Lee, 33, who lived in Portersville, was found buried in a shallow grave near Iannarelli's Union Valley Road residence in Shenango Township. She had been shot several times in the chest.

When entering his plea, Iannarelli said he could not recall his wife's death. He did recall drinking, depression, and arguing with her on that day, however. Following the argument, he said, he went to his bedroom for a gun.

His next recollection is waking up in his yard and seeing his wife's foot protruding from a dirt pile.

After a while, Dad pleaded guilty to killing Mom. He was sentenced to five years in prison for Mom's murder. I remember thinking about that while I lived at Aunt Judith's. I wondered what that meant for me. I would be twelve years old when he was released. Would he be allowed to visit me then? I figured Aunt Judith would never allow it if she had any say. Would I go live with him again? Would we all go live with him again? Would I, would we, have a choice?

I wanted to live with him. I wasn't afraid of him like everyone else was. I suppose that was a child's way of seeing things, but I was a child. I remember looking forward to his release, thinking he might take me away from this unbearable situation in which I was living. Anything would have been better than living with Aunt Judith. But on the other hand, when I thought about the big picture of it all, I had conflicting feelings about it. After all, he did kill my mother. He must be a terrible and dangerous person, right?

On top of all of those feelings, I couldn't understand why he only got sentenced to five years for her murder. It seemed like a pretty light sentence for such a serious and impactful crime.

I tried to process those feelings, alone of course. I wanted to talk through them with someone, but there wasn't anybody. In the end, it didn't matter. Dad died when I was twelve, just before his release. And so that was that. He left me too.

It wasn't Aunt Judith who told me that Dad had died. I found out at church. Aunt Judith didn't go to church with us; she sent us on a bus each Sunday morning, so she wasn't there. One of the older girls pulled me aside after the service one day and told me. She even gave me the newspaper clipping about it. By the time I found out, the funeral was already over, and I didn't get to go. How could Aunt Judith not let me say goodbye to my dad? Regardless of anything he did, he was still a part of me. He was still my dad. I was once again confused, angry, and saddened. But this time, I also felt defeated. I felt utterly defeated, in fact, because now I knew I was truly stuck in my current living situation for what seemed like an eternity. Furthermore, it solidified the fact that I couldn't trust Aunt Judith to be there for me, under any circumstances. I mean, she hadn't really been there for me up to that point anyway, but this took it to a new level.

She didn't even tell me my dad had died? What an awful thing to keep from someone.

I didn't tell Aunt Judith that I knew about Dad. I was too mad at her. Plus, I knew I couldn't tell her or, again, I would get in trouble. One day, she asked me what I had found out about Dad. Only then did I reveal what I knew to her. As predicted, I got in trouble, this time for knowing and not telling her. I know what was really going on, though. She was mad because she had been trying to control my knowledge of the situation, and someone took that power away from her. She never liked losing her control in any situation.

Someone later told me that Aunt Judith had gone to Dad's funeral just to make sure he was actually dead. I found out later that at some point Dad had threatened to kill her too. I suppose, therefore, she needed the closure of knowing he was gone for good. But still…

The years I spent living with Aunt Judith after Dad's death are just a big blur, more of the same. Nothing changed, for better or worse. I just lived day to day, waiting for my time with her to come to an end.

Aunt Judith was, at her core, cold toward me. I don't know if she meant to be, and maybe, just maybe, it would hurt her feelings to hear me say that. No, scratch that. It wouldn't. She has an uncanny ability to emotionally detach, to sever ties without hesitation, to move throughout life as if certain people never existed in her life to begin with.

I know this about her because I learned that from her. She taught me that survival means keeping your distance. And you'll see that in the end, to survive, that's exactly what I did.

CHAPTER FOURTEEN

NO LONGER ALONE

One day, I met a new girl at school, Savannah. I think we met in ninth grade. She had transferred into our school from a private school. We were both in band; she played the flute, and I played the clarinet. I would go out of my way to talk to her, and to my surprise, she welcomed my presence. I started making it a point to sit with her every day in band, then we started sitting together at lunch. Our personalities were complete opposites. I remember always being up and about, out of my seat, getting in trouble, probably seeking attention, though I didn't see it that way at the time. Savannah, on the other hand, was calm, cool, and collected. We became the best of friends, inseparable, at least at school.

I wasn't allowed to go to her house or have her come to mine. I wasn't even allowed to call her on the phone. Back then, landlines were the only phone option, so our friendship existed almost entirely at school. Even so, we took as many of the same classes together as possible. She was in more advanced classes than I was, so we couldn't take all of them together, but we made it work. It wasn't that I wasn't smart enough for the harder classes; I just didn't want to do the extra work. I had enough going on in my life. I didn't need more to do by adding things on at school.

Savannah was the first classmate who truly felt like a friend to me. I shared my secrets with her, and she shared hers with me. Our friendship continued to grow. It brought me happiness, something

I hadn't really associated with school before. For the first time, I actually looked forward to going, not just because it got me away from Aunt Judith, but because Savannah would be there. Before her, I spent my days surrounded by classmates but still felt alone. Having someone to connect with changed everything.

But on the days Savannah wasn't there, I didn't know what to do with myself. I had become too attached to her, codependent on our friendship perhaps. The emptiness I endured was unbearable. Eventually, we figured out a solution. We started planning our absences together so we'd both miss school on the same days. We began skipping classes together, then whole days. We didn't always spend our skip days together, but I wasn't about to go to school without her.

At one point, I orchestrated our first, and only, "Wampum Skip Day." This didn't include Savannah, but it happened on one of the same days she was going to be absent. I think there were six of us from my neighborhood who skipped together that day, and it was so much fun. We walked down the railroad tracks that ran behind our homes, swam in the river, and even swung from a rope that was tied to a tree by an old railroad car. We ended up at my house, where we almost accidentally caught the house on fire by kicking a jug of gasoline off the porch. It was an unforgettable day.

One time, when we were older, Savannah and I ran away from home together with our boyfriends. We thought we had the perfect plan. We were going to all move into an apartment together and start really living our lives. We even went and looked at a few apartments. It turned out that our plan for independence was short-lived. Her parents came to get her, and that was the end of that. I went home with Savannah for a few days, but then Aunt Judith picked me up from school and took me back home with her.

Somewhere along the line, we learned about an unofficial rule, or perhaps it was official, I don't know, that if you missed more than 28 days of school in a single year, you couldn't move on to the next grade or graduate if you were a senior. I honestly have no idea where that number came from, who first mentioned it, or whether it was even accurate. Regardless, Savannah and I took it extremely seriously. It quickly became an important rule, one we couldn't risk ignoring.

In order to stay within this critical limit, we had to become strategic about when and how we missed our days. We couldn't simply take off whenever we pleased because we had also discovered that most absences needed to be accompanied by a written excuse from our parent or guardian in order to be considered excused. Fortunately, or perhaps unfortunately, I had become quite skilled at manipulation during all the years I'd lived with Aunt Judith, so creating realistic reasons for absences and forging signatures on excuses was practically second nature to me. At the time, I felt uniquely proud of this skill, and it certainly came in handy.

By the time we reached senior year, Savannah and I had perfected the art of tactical absenteeism. We were masters at timing each absence carefully and planning our stories with precision, always mindful of staying beneath that magic number. So, when the year wrapped up, our total missed days was exactly 27 and a half, not even an extra hour. We had been keeping a running count, so we knew all along just how close we were to that number. That extra half day dangled there, a real temptation, but we didn't want to take any chances.

Savannah was my saving grace. I was no longer alone.

CHAPTER FIFTEEN

THE BOYFRIEND

Then there was Patrick.

Patrick was my boyfriend, my first real boyfriend. I started dating him when I was 16. He was four years older than me, a friend of my cousin Kevin's. He lived right up the road. One day he was at my house with Kevin and he asked me out. He seemed nice, so I accepted. Some of my neighborhood friends made fun of me for dating him, but I didn't care. I liked him. He was the first boy to want to get to know me. He would ask me what I was thinking and what I was feeling. That was something new. He wanted to spend as much time with me as I did with him, and I loved that feeling.

He cared for me. He truly loved me.

Not only did Patrick love me, but his family welcomed me with open arms. They were always happy to see me, always warm and kind.

Patrick became the best part of my life. Before we started dating, I didn't think anybody would ever want to be my boyfriend. I didn't think I would ever find anybody who would care for me. I had convinced myself that I was unlovable. But with Patrick, those feelings disappeared. For the first time, I thought that maybe, just maybe, I was worth someone's time after all.

We spent as much time together as we possibly could. Every single day followed the same comforting, familiar rhythm. I'd wake up and head to school in the morning, counting down the minutes until dismissal. I'd get home around three in the afternoon, rush inside, change my clothes and quickly freshen up, and barely 15 minutes later, Patrick would arrive, pulling up outside the house to pick me up on his way home from work. Those afternoons and evenings together became a welcomed routine to me. I'd stay out with him as long as Aunt Judith allowed, stretching every minute until my strict nine o'clock curfew, never a second later, though I always wished I could steal just a little more time.

It felt as though there was hardly ever a day that went by that we weren't together. Being with Patrick was utterly consuming. He occupied my every thought, every breath, every heartbeat. The love I felt coming from him was unlike anything I had ever experienced or even imagined possible. It was as though I had spent my entire life hidden away in darkness, unnoticed, unheard, and suddenly, he arrived, bringing warmth and illumination, allowing me to be seen clearly for the very first time. It was as if, after enduring a lifetime of silence, someone had finally heard my voice loud and clear. This was exactly what I needed. In fact, I had never been more certain about anything in my life.

Patrick made me feel loved in ways I'd never known before. When I was with him, I felt wanted, cherished, accepted completely, significant in a way that I'd longed for so deeply. I willingly gave him every piece of myself, surrendering completely and trusting fully that he was the person I'd spend the rest of my life with. My mind held no doubts. He was the one. Nothing, I believed, could possibly tear us apart.

Then he left me.

He turned 21, and just like that, he left me.

Another person who had mattered deeply to me, another man who had gained my trust, simply vanished from my life without warning. No indication, no gentle hints, just an abrupt departure. It felt like an earthquake had shattered the ground beneath me.

That breakup absolutely crushed me. I was devastated beyond anything I had ever experienced before.

Patrick tried to reassure me, saying it wasn't my fault, that it had nothing to do with me personally. He explained that it was simply the age gap, the timing of our lives. He wanted to go out to bars, wanted to experience that life, the freedom, independence, and the excitement of adulthood. As an adult now, looking back, I understand his perspective. I can even empathize. But back then, trapped in the raw intensity of heartbreak, I couldn't comprehend how he could do that to me. He knew the depth of my losses. He knew exactly what I had been through and how difficult it was for me to trust another person. He understood my vulnerabilities, my insecurities, and all my weaknesses because I had revealed them to him openly. I had bared my very soul to him, and yet, despite knowing all this, he still walked away.

It was the worst pain I had ever felt.

That breakup changed something fundamental inside of me. It wasn't just heartbreak; it was a confirmation of something I had already begun to suspect deep down: I couldn't truly count on anybody but myself. Every single person I'd ever allowed myself to trust or depend on had left me in one way or another. First my mom, then my dad, followed by my brothers and my sisters. And now, the person I'd believed with all my heart was the love of my life walked away. Left me behind, alone.

Once again, I found myself feeling lost, confused, defeated, and this time, profoundly alone. It seemed impossible to believe it was happening again. In the crushing weight of that loneliness, I made a promise to myself. Right then, in that moment of despair, I decided firmly and clearly that I would never again allow myself to be put in such a vulnerable position. I would never let someone else hold that kind of power over me. I didn't yet know exactly how I would achieve that, how I could shield my heart and protect myself from further pain, but I knew I had to figure it out. Somehow, I'd find a way.

In the months that followed our breakup, I tried my best to move forward. I dated a few different people, tested the waters, tried to distract myself and find a way to heal. It was enjoyable enough at times, and I tried to convince myself I was having fun, but none of those connections ever filled the void Patrick had left behind. After all, I wasn't about to truly open myself up to any of them. I missed Patrick deeply, painfully, and constantly, even when I pretended I didn't.

One afternoon, my cousin Amy and I decided to walk to the candy store, enjoying the warm sunshine and simple pleasure of being together. On our way home, when we passed by Patrick's house, I noticed his truck was in the driveway, which of course meant that he was home. My heart skipped a beat, as he was just a few feet away behind those walls. A pang of sadness washed over me as I confessed softly to Amy just how much I still missed him. Instead of sympathizing, Amy stopped dead in her tracks, turned sharply toward me, and urged me to go back and see him. Her words startled me, and my stomach instantly knotted with anxiety.

At first, I hesitated, flooded with doubts. Why would he want to see me? Wouldn't he have moved on by now? What on earth would I even say to him? But Amy was persistent, urging me onward and convincing me to at least try, to be brave, even if I was unsure. Her determination eventually became contagious, giving me just enough courage to take a deep breath, turn around, and slowly approach his house.

My heart raced as I walked up the driveway and knocked gently on his door. Each second of silence felt like an eternity as I stood there, pulse quickening, wondering what his response would be. Then the door swung open, and there he was, Patrick, standing right in front of me. When he saw it was me, his eyes lit up and a wide smile spread across his face, genuine and warm. He was happy to see me, and in that instant, I felt a rush of relief, joy, and hope all at once.

It turned out that he'd missed me too. We started talking again, slowly at first, cautiously testing the waters, rebuilding trust step by careful step. And before too long, almost inevitably, we found ourselves drawn back to one another, back together, almost as if we had never parted at all.

CHAPTER SIXTEEN

THE BROKEN CHAINS

Aunt Judith was the one who helped me get my very first job. She worked at a local retirement home, and soon enough, I was hired there too, serving food to the residents. It turned out to be a really nice job. It felt good to help others. I genuinely enjoyed seeing the smiles on the residents' faces as I brought them their meals each day. For the first time in my life, I had my very own money, and it felt amazing. I discovered quickly how empowering it was to have something I'd earned entirely on my own. It gave me a sense of freedom I had never experienced before, like I finally had a little bit of a say in how certain things could unfold in my life. It might not have been a lot, but that little bit of money was mine, and it meant everything to me.

After working there for a little while, I started thinking about how much fun it would be to have a job alongside Savannah, my best friend. She had just gotten hired at Burger King and always talked about how much fun it was. I didn't want to miss out, so I decided to apply too. When I found out I'd been hired, I was beyond excited, thrilled even, because now Savannah and I could see each other not only at school but also while we worked. Every shift became a chance for us to laugh, talk, and make memories, even while we were busy serving burgers and fries.

Having a job meant that slowly but surely, I was able to save a little bit of money. It wasn't long before I had saved up enough money to make the biggest purchase of my life: my very own car. I still remember the day vividly. I bought a 1980 Pontiac LeMans from a little gas station car lot just up the street from my house. The car cost me exactly $350, money I had proudly earned and carefully saved up. It was an old vehicle, painted a faded shade of blue, with plenty of wear and tear. The interior roof liner drooped down so low it almost touched my head when I drove, but none of that bothered me in the slightest. I simply bought a pack of colorful pushpins and used them to hold the sagging fabric up in place. Every pushpin I pressed into that roof liner felt symbolic. It was my way of taking control, piece by piece, bit by bit.

That car wasn't just a car to me. It was my ticket to independence, my way out from underneath Aunt Judith's controlling grip. For the first time, I could go where I wanted and when I wanted, without needing permission or relying on someone else's goodwill. With each mile I drove, each pushpin that held up the fabric above my head, I was silently declaring my newfound freedom. This was my life now, my path forward, and nobody could take that away from me.

Things were looking up. I had a job, I had some money, I had a boyfriend, and now I had a car.

CHAPTER SEVENTEEN

TESTING THE WATERS

The older I got, the more defiant I became toward my aunt and her rules. I decided I wanted to see my sister, Haylee. I knew I wasn't allowed, but I decided I was going to see her anyway. I had gone there once or twice with Aunt Judith, so I thought I had a pretty good idea of where she lived. I drove to her house and knocked on the door. I was so excited, and I knew she would definitely be happy to see me. I had a huge smile on my face while I waited for her to answer the door. That excitement was short-lived, though. It turned out I wasn't even at the right house; I was at my cousin Kelly's house. I guess I didn't know my way to her house after all. Never fear, though, Kelly called Haylee, who lived close by, and told her I was on my way over. Kelly gave me the directions, and off I went.

Finally, I could spend some time with my sister. I pulled up to her house and was filled with anticipation. I knocked on the door and stood there, wide-eyed with excitement. When Haylee opened the door, she paused and then got a huge smile on her face. She invited me in and gave me a big hug. Her hug felt like safety and security, like my worries and sadness were being transferred onto her. And I was right. Haylee was happy to see me.

That was the first of many visits with my sister. We talked about everything and anything; nothing was off-limits, but I held back some things. I didn't tell her everything. It was such a sense of freedom, being able to talk to a family member and not hide my feelings. Not having to worry about saying things a certain way so as to appease the listener and not being told that my thoughts, behaviors, and ideas were wrong. It was just me talking and sharing with my sister. This relationship held an unconditional love that the absence of contact with each other did not taint. I was starving for this connection. I thought that this must be what it's like to actually be part of a family.

In addition to sneaking away to see my sister, I started staying away from home more in general. Sometimes I would spend the whole weekend out and never check in with Aunt Judith. I was mostly working and staying with Savannah, but Aunt Judith didn't know that. About a month after I turned 18, my aunt confronted me. I had just returned to the house after not coming home for the weekend. There was a landing right inside the front door of the house; she met me there. She was angry but calm when she spoke. Her main complaint was that she found out I had been spending time with my sister. She told me I could either knock off my behaviors or I could get out.

One thing I haven't mentioned up to this point is how I couldn't see myself ever being able to leave Aunt Judith's house. Even though I pushed the boundaries, the control she had over me was incredible; I didn't know how I would ever be able to escape it.

I paused for about five seconds, processing her words: comply or get out. Little did she know, those words were music to my ears. That huge weight I had been carrying around since shortly after I moved in with her began to lift off my shoulders. Her judgment, her belittling, all the things that had made me feel like I was worthless, unlovable, and like I had no control over my own life, started to vanish from my body. The thought of leaving that controlling, manipulative, abusive, unloving home gave me an immediate sense of freedom. Up until that point, the thought of leaving felt impossible; the weight of her control over me had been so great that the thought of telling her I was moving out was numbing. Now I didn't have to worry about it.

I think she thought those words would scare me, perhaps into submission, but they definitely did not. I ran right upstairs, packed all of my belongings, stuffed them into my LeMans, and drove away. I was free. Finally.

As I pulled away, I watched Aunt Judith's house grow smaller and smaller in the rearview mirror. I wasn't running away; I was driving toward something better. Aunt Judith taught me how to cut people out of my life, and that's exactly what I did. I cut her out.

CHAPTER EIGHTEEN

THE WELCOMING

As I stepped out of Aunt Judith's house for the last time, a strange sensation washed over me, an incredible release, like I had finally exhaled after holding my breath for years. I felt lighter, as if the unbearable weight I had carried for so long had suddenly lifted. I didn't look back. I didn't want to. There was nothing there for me. It was time to look forward.

My hands gripped the steering wheel a little tighter as I replayed everything in my head, the fights, the indifference, the feelings of never belonging. Gone. All those feelings were behind me. But I didn't have time to dwell on it. I had to figure out what was next.

For a brief moment, as I drove away, I thought about Mom and Dad. I imagined that they would never have been OK with me being treated the way that I was while living in Aunt Judith's home and that they would never have made me so miserable that I would want to move out. I longed for the love I lost when Mom died.

I drove straight to Patrick's house, still absorbing the fact that I was free.

Patrick's family welcomed me instantly. They didn't hesitate. They didn't question. They just took me in. His mother, Fran, had two houses, one at the bottom of the hill where she ran a personal care home for the elderly, and another two houses up across the street where Patrick and his dad stayed. I was offered a place to stay, a routine, and most importantly, a home.

That first night, as I laid down in bed, I felt something I hadn't felt in years: peace. No tension. No fear of saying or doing the wrong things. Just warmth, comfort, and quiet. The kind of quiet that didn't feel heavy or lonely, but safe. I slept better that night than I had in a long time.

Living with Patrick's family was nothing like what I was accustomed to. There was kindness here, encouragement, a sense that I wasn't just tolerated, but truly cared for. Fran noticed things about me. She asked about my day. She wanted to know me, my thoughts, my dreams, my fears. She celebrated my small wins, whether it was a good grade or simply remembering to take care of myself.

She taught me things too, how to bake, how to cook, even basic things about proper hygiene that no one had ever thought to teach me before. I had been raised in survival mode. Fran was showing me how to live in comfort and security.

For the first time in my life since I moved back to Pennsylvania, I felt like I belonged. Like I wasn't a burden. Like I wasn't unwanted. Like I was home.

When I graduated from high school, something unexpected happened. Haylee, Brian, and Lisa, my siblings, came to celebrate with me. All four of us, together, for the first time since Mom died.

I couldn't believe they were there. I hugged each of them tightly, taking in their warmth, memorizing the way it felt to be surrounded by them again. For a brief moment, the years of separation melted away, and I felt like a kid again, a kid who had a family, a kid who mattered.

Fran threw me a graduation party. A giant cake, laughter, people who genuinely cared. It was surreal. I thought, "This was what family was supposed to feel like."

CHAPTER NINETEEN

KEEP IT HIDDEN

I found myself in a place now that, surprisingly to me, I didn't know how to handle. I hadn't learned to thoughtfully make my own decisions; I had simply gone through each day doing what was expected of me or doing what would make my life the most bearable. I had struggled through the past ten years being "on guard," in reactive mode. My feelings hadn't mattered for such a long time; I hadn't been heard for ten years. I presented to those around me as if I had a grip on things, but I didn't. Deep down, I was trying to figure things out along the way, knowing that I couldn't fail because there was no one to catch me. I was confident in my decisions, but that was because I didn't know what I didn't know and because I didn't really have anything to lose; life couldn't get any worse. I hadn't learned to see the big picture in situations, to analyze the data from all sides, and to act accordingly with purpose. Instead, it was ingrained in me to make the moves that would serve me best in the moment and to figure out the rest as time went on. There wasn't any situation that I couldn't handle because I had already overcome so much worse.

A defense mechanism I used, unknowingly, was that I was always wondering and planning for what was next instead of living in and appreciating the moments I was currently experiencing. I had been raised on survival, not on love. Current moments were never enough; they were never the end game. I always had to be thinking of and preparing for my next steps. This is how I lived for ten years, so how would I know that I needed to make a change in the way I processed information? How could I learn to function with a whole new mindset? How could I accept that now maybe somebody did care about my feelings?

Up to this point, in every situation I had experienced, through every heartbreak I had felt, every ridicule I had endured, every sadness I had undergone, I learned that I had to deal with my feelings alone. Countless times I would look to the heavens and ask, "Why did you take my Mom?" and I would imagine her helping me through whatever it was I was facing; furthermore, I would imagine that I wouldn't be facing it if she were still here. I learned to handle the feelings well, to tell myself I shouldn't be feeling what I was feeling, and to hide them from everyone around me. I had mastered detachment while craving connection. I grew up knowing that nobody cared about what I was going through and recognized that I was the only person who could take care of me. I learned it well, so well that I didn't want to let anybody in. I couldn't risk giving somebody the opportunity to break me again.

To this day, to an extent, I continue to hide my feelings. When I'm sad, when I'm angry, when I feel rejected, I bury it. When I'm hurt, I brush it off. I keep these feelings well hidden from those around me. Instead, I smile, I push through, and I encourage others not to feel this way. But inside, it builds up. It gathers in a pocket of self-loathing that I set space aside for as a child. Nobody sees it, but it's there. Those feelings are only for me to know about; I don't share them with anyone. Sometimes, when they're bursting from the small chamber they stay hidden in, I remove myself from everyone else and let them out. I sob, with tears flowing down my face. I replay all of the hurts that are leaving my body through this expression of defeat. I do this alone; I've always felt my feelings alone. Then, when I've let it all out, I pull myself together, put the smile back on my face, and return to life. Nobody ever knows.

CHAPTER TWENTY

IN THEIR ABSENCE

As I settled into my new life, something kept tugging at me, a quiet but persistent ache deep within my chest. It was the profound absence of my dad's family, the family I had once known but had been forced to forget.

For years, they had been kept from me, deliberately pushed out of my life. I'd grown up hearing endless stories that painted them as villains, dangerous people who were somehow involved with and/or happy about my mom's death. Aunt Judith had whispered these dark suspicions into my ear so often they had become a part of me. But as I grew older, doubts crept in, twisting through my mind like ivy around an old fence. Were these stories even true? Were any parts of them true? Or was this just another example of Aunt Judith's manipulative tactics, another way she had found to control me, to isolate me from anyone who might show me the truth or maybe some affection?

I didn't have the answers I longed for, and maybe I never would. But one thing was clear to me: I missed my dad's family deeply. Or perhaps it wasn't even them specifically I missed. Maybe it was the idea of them. The memories of warmth, the echoes of laughter shared around kitchen tables, the faint recollection of feeling loved, welcomed, and completely accepted in their presence. It felt like a distant dream now, blurred by time, clouded by uncertainty, yet still powerful enough to tug insistently at my heart.

Eventually, I decided to reach out. My wedding day was approaching, and the thought of embarking on such a significant moment in my life without at least attempting to reconnect felt unbearably lonely. So, gathering all my courage, I took a chance and extended an invitation.

I wasn't even sure if they'd want to come. After so many years apart, would they still care? On top of that, I didn't even know how to get in touch with most of them. Their addresses and phone numbers weren't something I ever had; I was a young child when I had last seen them. Still, I reached out to the few whose information I was able to find and asked them to pass the word along to others.

CHAPTER TWENTY-ONE

WEDDING DAY, WITHOUT MOM

The day was finally here. The sun was shining, the church was decorated, and the "Just Married" sign was being placed on our exit car. Everything was perfect. Almost.

I didn't have my mother.

The weight of her absence was heavier on me that day than on any other.

I imagined her there beside me in a pretty gown, helping me get ready, telling me I looked beautiful. For a moment, I disappeared into a scene my mind was creating, enjoying every second with her, only to return to the reality of her void. I looked out the window and up at the sky, as if to nod to Mom, to let her know I hadn't forgotten about her on this day. I paused, as if I was waiting for her response, as if I knew she was watching down on me from heaven.

Just as it was almost time for me to walk down the aisle, my cousin Stacy announced that Aunt Judith was on her way into the room. I was happily surprised. We hadn't really patched things up since I moved out, and she hadn't shown me much regard while I lived with her, but I thought maybe she was coming to help fill my mom's void. I anticipated her walking over to hug me, or to smile at me, or to tell me my mom would be so happy today. Something. I felt excitement when I saw her come in.

She glanced at me, then looked away. She asked where her daughter Heather was, as Heather was one of my bridesmaids. Then she turned and left the room.

That was it. She didn't show me one ounce of anything. She just left.

I felt her rejection all over again, hard. I couldn't hold in my sadness, my emptiness, my anger, my frustration. I started to cry. My sister Haylee, my cousin Stacy, and one of my bridesmaids saw what had happened. They came over, gave me a hug, and helped me pull myself together. They couldn't fix the situation, they couldn't undo the hurt Aunt Judith caused, they couldn't bring my mom back, but through their actions they showed me that they cared. Then they reminded me that today was about me, not Aunt Judith, and that my future husband was waiting in the other room.

As I gathered myself and made my way to the sanctuary, I thought about my mom, and I smiled. I thought about my future husband, and I smiled. I thought about my dad's family and told myself it would be okay if they hadn't come. I had already prepared myself for that disappointment.

As I stood in the doorway at the end of the aisle, arm in arm with my escort, ready for "Here Comes the Bride" to play, heart pounding, I looked around the room. My soon-to-be husband was eagerly and nervously waiting for me. My bridesmaids and the groomsmen were standing near him. The pastor was in place. Everyone in the sanctuary stood up. All eyes were on me.

Then I saw my dad's family.

They had come. One by one, faces I hadn't seen in so long they felt almost like ghosts stepping out of the shadows of my past. Their familiar smiles. Their eyes filled with cautious sentiment. They were there, in that church, for me.

My heart skipped a beat, my knees went weak, and I gripped my escort's arm just a bit tighter.

Throughout the day there were so many things I wanted to say, so many questions I wanted to ask, but it was my wedding day, and time slipped quickly through my fingers. Even though we didn't exchange many words, their presence spoke volumes. It filled a space in my heart that had stood painfully empty for so many years.

Despite everything that had happened, it wasn't too late. They were there. And that was enough.

CHAPTER TWENTY-TWO

THE BUILDING OF OUR NEST

Life was finally moving forward. Patrick and I were married. I was attending college. Next on my list was something I had wanted more than anything; children, a family of my own.

But something deep inside me whispered that it wouldn't happen.

There was no logical reason to think I couldn't have a baby, or several babies. But after everything I had been through, I just couldn't imagine that something so beautiful could come together for me.

One night, I had a dream I would never forget. In the dream, I gave birth to a baby girl. I didn't hold her. I didn't touch her. I just looked at her, mesmerized. She was perfect.

I couldn't get that dream out of my head. I longed for that stick to turn blue.

To my surprise, A short time later, it did! That dream became reality. I was pregnant. I was going to be a mother! I told everyone who would listen. I couldn't wait for my belly to grow, for the world to see this miracle.

I imagined what it would be like when this blessing arrived; snuggling together, pouring over the baby's tiny little fingers and tiny little nose, caressing the softness of the skin, taking in the new-baby scent. I drifted off into thinking about Mom, and how she was missing the birth of this grandchild. I imagined what it would be like to have Mom around during my pregnancy, to ask her questions, to be comforted on days I doubted my ability to be a mother. The thoughts were blissful.

That joyousness was short-lived.

One morning, I woke up and knew something was wrong. Patrick rushed me to the hospital. As we waited in the emergency room, I gripped his hand, searching his face for reassurance, but I could see it, the same fear I felt, reflecting right back at me.

After what seemed like hours, the doctor confirmed what we already knew. I had miscarried.

I had lost a lot in my life, but nothing, *nothing,* had ever hurt like this. Patrick held me as I sobbed. He cried too. We were both so broken over the loss of this precious life.

I fell into a darkness I didn't know how to escape. I asked God how He could do this to me. Hadn't I been through enough? And then, the thoughts I had worked so hard to bury came rushing back. That old voice, the one that had whispered to me in Aunt Judith's house, was back, but in a different rhealm. *You don't deserve this. You were never meant to have a baby. You aren't good enough. This is your fault.* I didn't know if anyone around me could see it, but inside, I was plummeting.

I continued to push through each day, with a smile on my face, as always, hiding the hurt that was buried inside me. In June of the following year, I found out I was pregnant again. The joy was instant, but so was the fear. I was ecstatic and also utterly petrified. What if I lost this baby too? What if something was wrong? Every ache, every twinge, every soreness sent me spiralling. I called the doctor constantly, desperate for reassurance. He earned every penny during that pregnancy.

The following February, after months of waiting, worrying, and praying, I gave birth to the most beautiful creation I had ever seen, a healthy baby girl, Maria.

The moment I saw her, everything changed. The love that consumed me was wondrous, overwhelming, unlike anything I had ever felt before or even imagined. As I held her, all of my feelings of hopelessness and inadequacy, along with my concerns that I was not good enough to deserve her, vanished. When I looked at her beautiful features, saw how content she was, and gazed into her tiny little eyes while she gazed back at me, I knew that everything was as it should be; and that we would be okay.

She doesn't know it, but she saved me. She was the best thing that had ever happened to me in my entire life.

CHAPTER TWENTY-THREE

MOTHERLESS MOTHERING

loved being a new mother. I dreamt of giving Maria everything I had missed out on as a child. I had weathered my painful childhood and was determined to raise her in a positive, loving, and encouraging environment. I dressed her in nice, clean clothes, not like the dirty ones I wore as a child. I took her everywhere I could with me and showed her off. I poured every ounce of myself into ensuring that she was well cared for. I vowed to never let her be placed in a situation where she would witness or be the victim of abuse, ridicule, or loneliness. I surrounded her with people who loved her, cherished her, and wanted only the best for her. She was the apple of my eye, my reason for being. But something was missing, something I couldn't replace, something that I had longed for since that harrowing day when I was seven years old: the presence of my own mother.

Being a new mom without having my own mom around was difficult, to say the least. I didn't have her to seek guidance from when I had questions. I couldn't gain wisdom from her. She wasn't there to tell me that situations were normal when all of the voices inside my head were telling me they weren't, that I was messing it up. Mostly, though, she wasn't there to hold Maria when she cried or to hold me when I felt defeated by this precious life that was entrusted to me. I faced every new situation blindly. I wanted my mom; I needed my mom. I felt that emptiness stronger as a mom than I had ever felt it before.

Don't get me wrong, Fran and the rest of Patrick's family were wonderful with Maria and me.

By the time Maria was born, Patrick and I had our own home about three miles away from his parents. Any time I started to feel overwhelmed, I'd load Maria up into the car and drive to Fran's house. I didn't have to say a word; Fran could tell what I needed just by looking at me. She would take Maria into her arms, and I would instantly feel better, reassured that everything was going to be okay. It was as if Fran had a connection with me that allowed her to take my worries away and fill me with peace.

Although I had emotional support from Patrick's family, there wasn't a day that went by that I didn't feel the absence of my mother and imagine how things would be if she were still alive. I was angry at my dad for taking her from me.

Shortly after Maria's birth, one of my older cousins from my dad's side stopped by my house to visit us. It was nice that he came, but I didn't really invite him inside. He stood in the doorway during our short conversation. Honestly, I felt uneasy. Looking back, I realize there was no reason to worry, but it had been deeply ingrained in me to be cautious around anyone from my dad's side of the family. I was taught they were dangerous and that they had assisted in my mother's murder. Despite that lingering worry, I genuinely wanted him and all of my dad's family around because I didn't truly believe what I had been told. As I continued on my journey to get to know them, I battled an internal struggle between the caution that had been drilled into me and the kindness they showed me through their actions.

Around the same time, Patrick and I took Maria to visit another cousin. The visit went well; he shared pictures and stories about different family members and seemed genuinely happy that we were there.

Small visits like these kept occurring, and I continued to seek connections with my dad's family.

Then, when Maria was four months old, we discovered I was pregnant again. This wasn't by accident; Patrick and I planned for this baby. Our family was growing quickly, and we couldn't have been happier. I was excited for baby number two and eager to share my love with another child. We were building the family I had always longed for.

CHAPTER TWENTY-FOUR

AWARENESS

One day at college, shortly after learning about this new pregnancy, I suddenly realized the world around me was much larger than the pain, hurt, and death I'd grown up knowing, the very things Patrick had rescued me from. I was encountering new people, embracing new ideas, and discovering opportunities I never knew existed. I realized I had choices and, most importantly, the freedom to make decisions for myself, not just go with what worked for me that day. It dawned on me that there was more to life than what I'd known.

See, that's the issue when, at your core, you're used to feeling unloved. You cling to anyone who shows you affection without discerning if they're truly what's best for you. You just know someone loves you, and you don't want to return to a time when nobody did.

I loved Patrick, but I was missing out on so much that I'd never even known existed due to my upbringing. I had unintentionally settled because I didn't realize I had options; nobody had ever chosen me first. Additionally, to be honest, in the back of my mind, I always wondered if Patrick would leave me again, as I'd never truly healed from the hurt of him leaving abruptly when he turned 21.

For these reasons, I decided to end our marriage. It was not an easy decision or an easy conversation to have with him or his family, but staying together wasn't fair to either one of us. It had to be done.

Patrick and I divorced.

Making this drastic change, leaving the warmth and security I had in my marriage and starting over, wasn't easy. I felt incredibly guilty about this decision; I still do, even today. I've heard it said that hurt people hurt people, and I believe it. That's exactly what happened. I was hurt and damaged. Patrick wasn't the problem; I was. I pulled him into the dysfunction of my life and caused him pain. I'm truly sorry that I did that to him, to his family, and to our two children; but I am eternally grateful for the two beautiful children we share.

I knew that if I wanted a different life, I needed to take control of my situation and make changes. So that's what I did. I cut everyone out of it: Aunt Judith, family members, neighborhood friends, and Patrick's family, though I never cut Patrick from our children's lives. I moved away, both physically and emotionally. I focused solely on my schooling, my beautiful daughter, and my newly discovered pregnancy. I left, and I never turned back.

CHAPTER TWENTY-FIVE

THE NEW HORIZON

It was done. I had left behind the family I grew up with, the husband and in-laws I had married into, and the town that held no friends to tether me there. That part was easy; there was nothing to keep me. What I needed was to escape, to break free from the life I had endured for the past fifteen years.

It's important to note that it wasn't my cousins I was leaving behind, not intentionally. I loved them, and I still do. It wasn't about them. It was about the weight of that life and the suffocating feelings that came with it. I needed space to find myself, to figure out who I really was without the echoes of my past defeating me. And I knew one thing for sure: I couldn't stay in that life and discover myself at the same time.

As I left that life behind, I felt like I was standing at the edge of a cliff, stepping off into the unknown. But the air felt lighter. The silence, clearer. For the first time, no one was telling me who I was or who I wasn't. For the first time, I belonged to myself.

I never questioned myself about whether or not I was making the right move; I knew I was. Also, I always knew I didn't have a plan B. I didn't have anybody to fall back on. It was up to me to provide for me and my babies. I always knew that if I wanted a different kind of life than what I was raised in, I needed to remove myself from what I knew, and I needed to make positive changes for my own well-being.

My personal drive to be the best I could be is something I've carried with me all along. I think it has a lot to do with not having what I needed growing up, yet yearning for it.

I moved to Sharon, PA so I could be close to my sister, Haylee. I got an apartment about a block away from her. I asked my future second husband, Vincent, if he wanted to move in with me. He did. Vincent also saw me for who I was, but on a different, deeper level. He was interested in everything about me. When I told him things about myself, he questioned them so he could understand what I was feeling. Then he took those feelings and carried them as his own, to the point where he understood every word I said, even every word I didn't say, as if he had experienced or was experiencing the same things. I could be across the room in a group of people, and he could tell by the look on my face, a comment I made, or a glance in his direction exactly what I was feeling and needing in that moment. He would then act on that knowledge to make the situation what I needed it to be. We were a team. I found a friendship in him that I never knew could exist, a deep, caring, and loving friendship. He was my soulmate, truly.

My second child, Patrick Jr., was born the following spring. Patrick Sr. was at the hospital with me for his birth, of course. It was an easy delivery. Patrick Jr. looked so much like his dad; he still does. The love we both had instantly for this tiny infant was immense. Even though Patrick Sr. and I were no longer together, we put that aside and poured all of our love into our brand-new baby boy.

So, there I was, a single mom in college with two little kids and Vincent by my side.

We lived in the apartment in Sharon for about a year before we started looking for more permanent housing. I didn't have much, but I wasn't used to having much, so it didn't matter. Honestly, it never felt like I didn't have much anyway because I had the love of Vincent, I had my babies, and I was continuing to move forward in life. I was always looking ahead at how I could make my situation better.

Vincent and I found a trailer in a trailer park in Grove City. It seemed like a nice town, and I didn't have roots anywhere anyway, so the location didn't really matter. This seemed like a nice next step, which was exactly what I needed.

The cost of the trailer was around $8,000. I used my student loans to pay cash for it. Not the best financial move, but at the time, it was a lifesaver. I felt triumphant when I walked into that home, knowing it was mine and nobody could take it away from me. I had left a manipulative, unloving, and demeaning environment where I had no control. Now, as I walked into this new home, I knew that I had provided a space that was mine, a space that I could fill with love, encouragement, and uplifting support for my children. Again, the cycle of emotional abuse and neglect ended with me.

CHAPTER TWENTY-SIX

UNLEASHING MY POTENTIAL

I felt like I was doing pretty well for myself and my babies. I had Vincent by my side, and I didn't have to worry about housing or providing for my family. I could just focus on loving my babies, working, and earning my college degree.

While attending college, I secured a job at a supercenter in New Castle, PA. It was a brand-new store, new people, new challenges. I applied, but I didn't really think I would be chosen for a position. After all, I was used to being rejected, and this was something I really wanted. To my surprise, though, I was hired. I couldn't believe it. I started out as a part-time cashier. I gave that job my all, and it paid off. It didn't take me long to get promoted to a customer service manager and then to the lead customer service manager. My supervision team saw something in me, which motivated me to work even harder. They saw that I had drive, was dedicated, and was able to solve problems quickly and efficiently.

It felt strange to have people notice the positives in me. I soaked it in, and I thrived on getting more of it.

I was approached numerous times about going into the company's management program, but I declined. On one hand, I knew that it would be a positive move for me because I knew I would continue to grow in the company and earn promotions, which, of course, meant better pay and a better lifestyle for my family. But on the other hand, I knew I had two little kids at home, and as a manager, my schedule would be more demanding, taking even more time away from them than I was already sacrificing.

As lead customer service manager, I was in charge of writing the schedule for everyone under me, around 140 employees, plus my own schedule. I had so much going on in my life that it was nice to be able to write my own schedule. I scheduled my college classes on Monday, Wednesday, and Friday mornings. I worked late on Mondays and Fridays, so I didn't really see the kids on those days, which was hard. I worked early on Tuesdays and was off on Wednesdays and Thursdays. This gave me an uninterrupted block of time with the kids. I worked early on Saturdays and Sundays and had the evenings with the kids. Basically, I scheduled myself in a way that would maximize my time with the kids, to the best of my ability.

It may seem like a lot, juggling work, school, and the kids, but it wasn't. I didn't see it as a difficult task; it wasn't overwhelming in any way. Instead, it was me figuring out how to make my life work in a way that helped my family move forward, to provide them with better than what I had. It was a blessing to have the ability to make these decisions.

I graduated from the local community college with my associate's degree and then transferred to a nearby university, where I eventually earned my bachelor's degree in elementary education. It wasn't easy. Some days, when I was pregnant with Patrick Jr., I would have to take Maria to school with me. It wasn't ideal, but I didn't have a choice. I remember taking naps in the car between classes while Maria slept in her car seat; I was so tired. When it was time to complete my student teaching, I had to figure out childcare for both kids for the full 16-week semester. I was already taking the semester off work. Vincent had to cover the bills, so he couldn't take off work too. I didn't have anybody to help me; I only had myself and Vincent.

I remember thinking, if Mom were still alive, she would help me.

I had to think outside the box. I made an arrangement with a Christian daycare/preschool. They would watch the kids for me while I was student teaching in exchange for me paying a small weekly fee and working at the daycare after school until closing time. To put this into perspective, I would get up and get the kids ready each morning, drive 45 minutes to the daycare for a 6:30 a.m. drop-off, drive another 45 minutes to the school where I was student teaching, teach all day, drive back to the daycare, work for two hours, then drive home. That, of course, was in addition to preparing my lessons for school, cooking dinner, and tending to the things that needed to be done at home. It was a busy schedule, but I never felt defeated by it, and I never complained; I was grateful to find a daycare that would work with me.

When I graduated with my bachelor's degree, Maria was four and Patrick was three. It was really difficult to find teaching jobs in the Grove City area back then, as we were surrounded by three major teacher-producing colleges. Unless you had connections, which I definitely did not, local employment seemed practically impossible. I was offered a teaching position in North Carolina, which I had planned to accept, but Vincent didn't want to move away from his parents, so I declined and we stayed in Grove City.

Around that same time, I organized our first family reunion, Dad's side, of course. I made contact with everyone I could and set up the event. I remember that I made several Jell-O mold desserts, which I was really proud of, and shared them with everyone. We had a fantastic turnout, and I was elated. At that reunion, I remember thinking that it felt as though I had found everyone again, but the truth was that they hadn't been lost; I had. I was so disconnected from everyone that I even asked each person to wear a name tag because I didn't know who anybody was. The reunion made me feel like things were finally coming together. This gathering became the first of many reunions, laying a strong foundation for the relationships I was so desperately longing for.

CHAPTER TWENTY-SEVEN

THE DAWN OF A NEW DAY

Maria started kindergarten later that year, and because I'd always tried to be as involved with the kids as possible, I became a Girl Scout leader. I had the best little Daisy Girl Scouts ever; we had such a wonderful time. One of the mothers, Karen, was especially friendly, and we quickly formed a bond. Over the year, our friendship grew stronger. Karen told me about her role as a house parent at a local residential treatment facility, where she cared for boys who were placed in her home. She mentioned that the facility was looking for more house parents.

Excited by the opportunity, I spoke to Vincent about it. We agreed that this was something we couldn't pass up. Vincent and I had previously discussed how unlikely it was that we would ever be able to afford our own house. We were managing, but we were living paycheck to paycheck. Becoming house parents seemed like an ideal solution, offering us stability and a chance to work at home together. However, there was one catch: we had to be married to qualify for the position.

Although Vincent and I weren't married yet, we had already been planning our wedding for later that year. We decided to officially marry sooner at the Justice of the Peace so we could apply for the job, but we still planned to have our regular wedding celebration months later.

This quick wedding was very low-key. We scheduled an appointment during Vincent's lunch break one day because he couldn't take time off work. The Justice of the Peace's office was conveniently located near his workplace. My sister Haylee joined us, along with my Aunt Martha and her husband.

Soon after we married, Vincent, Maria, Patrick, and I moved into the residential treatment facility. It was everything I had ever hoped for. I could work from home with my family by my side, care for the boys placed with us, whom we lovingly called "our boys," and, to top it all off, Karen lived there too. I felt I had it all: my family, meaningful work, and a true friend.

CHAPTER TWENTY-EIGHT

UNCOVERING THE BURIED STORY

Through everything I had gone through, I always carried a deep curiosity about my mom's death. Why did the tragedy that started this roller coaster of my life happen? What was the truth? How could I find it? These questions sat heavy on my chest, like stones. Why did Mom go alone to Dad's house? Was anybody else there that day with Dad? These weren't just missing details; they were pieces of a puzzle I had been carrying for years. I decided it was time to start seeing what I could find out.

Up until the time I moved into the residential treatment facility, the amount of information I had regarding my mom's death was very minimal. I didn't know who or what to believe because I had been told so many different things. I had heard that Mom's van was parked at the end of the road where our house was and that she had gone to Dad's house that day because he told her he was going to sell the house and needed her to sign some papers. I had heard that Dad shot her three times in the throat in the kitchen and then buried her in a hole beside the well by our house.

I was told that Dad wasn't the one who dug the hole, that he had someone else do it, that he told them he needed to "bury some trash."

That statement still disgusts me.

I had heard that Mom had gone to Dad's house that morning to sign the papers, alone. I was told that Dad admitted to killing Mom, then later said he didn't do it, then later admitted to it again. One person told me there was a trial. Others said there was not. I was told that Dad's family helped him carry out the crime, which I presume is why Aunt Judith didn't allow me to be around them, and that someone had even gone to the house to try to clean up afterward. I was told that my dad was very short, standing tall at 4'8", and that he had a bad back, so on a normal day there was no way he could drag or carry my mother's body from the kitchen to the hole in the yard by the well.

There were so many details that didn't add up. Why would my dad do such a thing? Why would anyone let Mom go there alone if it was so dangerous? Was there something actually wrong with my dad's family that justified me being kept away from them? Did Dad admit to it? Did Dad have help? What was going through Dad's mind?

And the even more pressing question, not that I expected to find the answer in any documentation: What about me? After all of this happened, after I was moved to Aunt Judith's home, why wasn't anybody checking in on me? Why didn't anyone come to see how I was, find out what was going on, save me from that house? Did everyone just forget about me? It sure felt like they did.

My need to get answers became all-consuming, as if knowing the truth would somehow undo the past. I decided I needed to do some research on my own. I needed to separate myself from the stories I had heard and look to where the information was in writing. So I went to the library, alone.

The library was an old building, quiet, with a stillness that almost felt sacred. The area where archived documents were kept was in the back of a large, nearly empty room. I remember the smell of aged paper and the sound of my footsteps on the floors as I made my way to the records section.

I spent hours upon hours, over months upon months, reading old newspaper articles and court documents. I combed through everything I could find, trying to piece together what really happened. Every time I uncovered something new, I would get lost in it, trying to imagine what it was like in those exact moments, trying to feel what each person had felt. The weight of it was unbearable at times. I would take breaks to gather myself, to cry. I didn't want to keep reading, but I couldn't stop. I needed to know.

Affidavit for Search Warrant

At approximately 20:02 hours August 12, 1980 Officer John Hart of the Shenango Township Police Department was summons upon call ariginating from a one William Gibson, that there had been a shooting on union valley road. Officer Hart went to the area of union valley road and was shown a site of fresh dirt at the south east corner of the house identified to him as the residence of Frank Ianarrelli by said Gibson and as well as ______ who was also at the scene. He was requested by ______ to examine the scene and upon doing so observed a shoe and foot protruding from the fresh dirt. Immediate examination with his hands revealed a body of a person partially covered with dirt and he would find no pulse upon testing for same. Officer Hart summons the County Corner and the Pennsylvania State Police by radio. ______, upon seeing the body uncovered stated to officer Hart that Frank Ianerelli had shot the victim and that the victim was Laura Ianerelli, wife of Frank, this statement was made in the presence of Frank Ianerrelli who was then detained as was ______ by Officer Hart.upon arrest 20:20 hours Tpr. Rodney Fowler advised Frank Ianerelli of his constitutional and legal rights and then asked him if he had killed his wife. He stated that he did kill her and that he did so by shooting her, that the gun he used was in the house and that the gun was a 22 caliber. He further stated the house there was his residence. The body was removed from fresh dirt at or about 22:15 hours by Corner Howard Reynolds while you affaint was present and a wound seeping blood was observed in her chest area. The body was revealed to be an adult female person and identified by ______ as Laura Ianerelli when he state he has knwon her for more than two years. Offiœer John Hart also identified the body as Laura Ianerelli and advided you affaint to be known her and his husband and known the house to be this property and the residence of Frank Ianerelli. He stated he has known the couple for at least five years and has visited them at the residence on prior calls. Your affaint observed Frank Ianerelli at the said residence, observed the body of Laura Ianerelli being removed from the shellow dirt, observed fresh blood in the shellow grave and freshly dug dirt. Frank Ianerelli stated to you affaint at the scene of his residence of or about 20:30 hours, the 12, of August , that he did shoot Laura Ianerelli with a 22 caliber weapon and that the weapon was in his house on the table, Your affaint verily believes all of the above and believes the said weapon is still in the residence of Frank Ianerelli and as well other evidence that will indicate the criminal activities of Frank Ianerelli on the 12th of August 1980 and the times there of , Therefore your affaint verily believes probable cause exsist for the issuance of a warrant to persue a search of the premises and residence of Frank Ianerelli on Union Valley road Shenango Township and request the service of same for the purpose. That your affaint observed parked in the yard of the above described premises a blue chevrolet stationwagon with PA registration No. 72590S whiœh was identified as to your affaint on the vehicle used by Frank Ianerelli admitts unto your affaint said vehicle was his own. Further the foresaid ______ stated that upon his attempting to locate Laura Ianerelli during the afternoon of August 12, 1980 he observed said stationwagon backed alongside the house to a point within a few feet of the shallow grave, were the body of Laura Ianerelli was found back in the mud near the gravesite indicated tire marks which appeared, upon inspection to have been made by the tires of the said station-wagon.

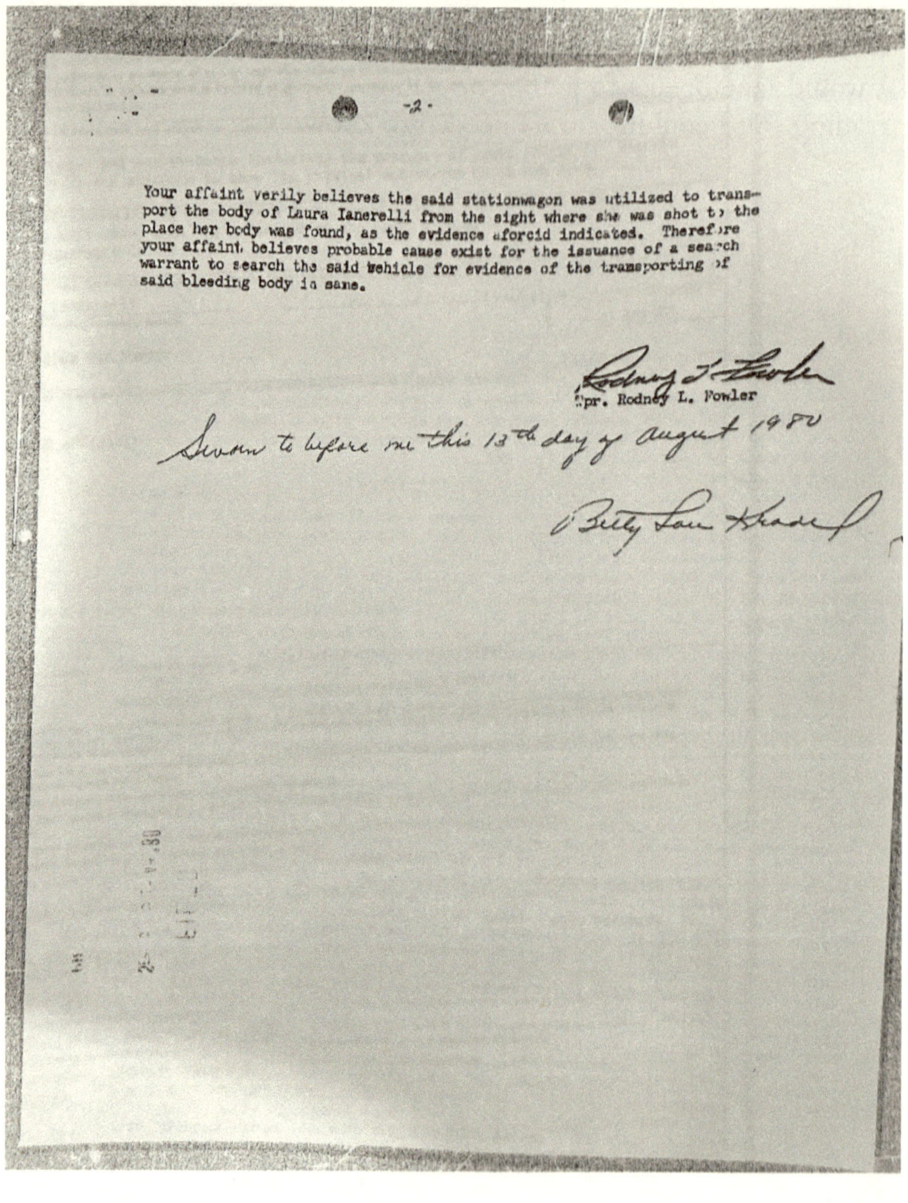

- 2 -

Your affaint verily believes the said stationwagon was utilized to transport the body of Laura Ianerelli from the sight where she was shot to the place her body was found, as the evidence aforcid indicates. Therefore your affaint believes probable cause exist for the issuance of a search warrant to search the said vehicle for evidence of the transporting of said bleeding body in sane.

Tpr. Rodney L. Fowler

Sworn to before me this 13th day of August 1980

...PY OF THIS FORM, WHEN COMPLETED, IS TO BE ATTACHED TO EACH COPY OF THE SEARCH WARRANTS/AFFIDAVIT

Commonwealth of Pennsylvania
COUNTY OF _Lawrence_ } SS:

RECEIPT/INVENTORY
OF SEIZED PROPERTY FROM

DATE OF SEARCH: _15 Aug 80_
INVENTORY CONTROL NO.: A 30386
TIME OF SEARCH: _11:05_ ☒ A.M. ☐ P.M.
SEARCH WARRANT NO.: _B37412_

Rodney L Fowler
(Name)

Penna State Police
(Address)

The following property was taken/seized and a copy of this Receipt/Inventory with a copy of the Search Warrant and affidavit(s) is ☐ personally served on the above named ☒ was left at (describe location at premises) _Frank C. Iannarelli_ _Residence_ as required by the Pennsylvania Rules of Criminal Procedure 2008(a)(b).

QUANTITY	ITEM DESCRIPTION	MAKE, MODEL, SERIAL No., COLOR, etc.
	KITCHEN. CHAIR. LIGHT GREEN WITH CROME LEGS.	
Two	12 BY 12 KITCHEN FLOOR TILE	
	BLOOD SAMPLE FROM LEG OF KITCHEN TABLE	

☐ CHECK HERE IF LISTING CONTINUED ON ADDITIONAL FORM SETS

We _TPR Rodney L Fowler_ of _Penna State Police_ swear (or affirm) that the property seized and taken pursuant to and under the authority of the above numbered Warrant is to the best of my/our knowledge and belief correctly and completely listed above as a just, true and complete Receipt/Inventory.

[signature] / _Rodney L Fowler_ / _360c_ / _TPR_
(Signature of Person Issuing Receipt/Inventory) (Printed Name of Person Issuing Receipt/Inventory) (Affiliation) (Badge No. or Title)

SIGNATURE OF WITNESS TO VERIFY ACCURACY OF INVENTORY IN ABSENCE OF OWNER/OCCUPANT OF PREMISES. (Rule 2009(a))

[signature] (Print name of Witness) (Address of Witness) ~ (Affiliation of Witness) (Badge No. or Title)

[signature] / _Rodney L Fowler_ / _PSP_ / _3600 TPR_
(Signature of Person Making Search) (Printed Name of Person Making Search) (Police Department/Unit/Affiliation) (Badge No. or Title)

Rule 2008(a). A law enforcement officer, upon taking property pursuant to a search warrant, shall leave with the person from whom or from whose premises the property was taken a copy of the Warrant and affidavit(s) in support thereof, and a receipt for the property seized. A copy of the Warrant and affidavit(s) must be left whether or not any property was seized.

Rule 2008(b). If no one is present on the premises when the Warrant is executed, the officer shall leave the documents specified in paragraph (a) at a conspicuous location in the said premises. A copy of the Warrant and affi...

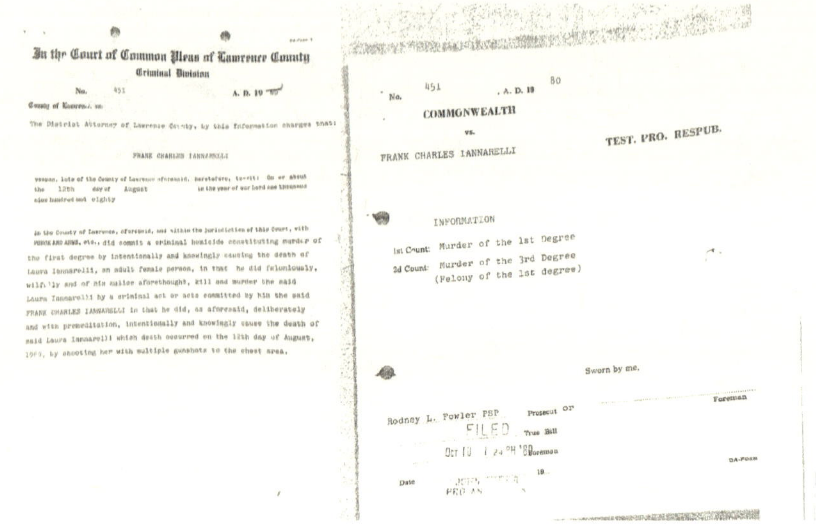

Dad pleaded not guilty, even though he initially admitted that he had killed her.

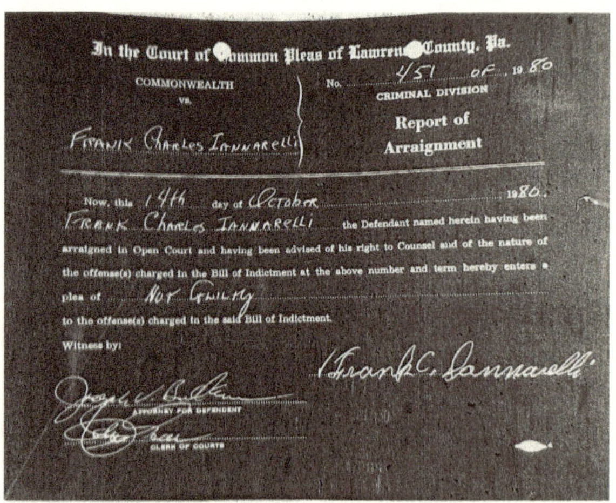

Since he was drunk when he made the admission and hadn't been read his rights, it was requested that his words not be permitted to be used against him.

COMMONWEALTH OF PENNSYLVANIA,
Plaintiff

v.

FRANK CHARLES IANNARELLI,
Defendant.

: IN THE COURT OF COMMON PLEAS
: LAWRENCE COUNTY, PENNSYLVANIA
: No. 451 of 1980   Criminal Division

DEFENDANT'S OMNIBUS PRE-TRIAL APPLICATION

TO THE HONORABLE, THE JUDGES OF THE SAID COURT:

AND NOW comes the Defendant, Frank Charles Iannarelli, by his attorneys, John R. Seltzer and Dominick Motto, Esquires, to file the within Omnibus Pre-Trial Application on behalf of the Defendant.

I. APPLICATION TO SUPPRESS STATEMENTS OF THE DEFENDANT

1. On August 12, 1980, the Defendant was arrested and by criminal Complaint filed the same date was charged with the offenses of criminal homicide and murder.

2. At the time of the Defendant's arrest, he was standing outside of his residence at Union Valley Road, Shenango Township, Lawrence County, Pennsylvania, at about 8:00 P.M. and was arrested by officers of the Shenango Township Police Department and the Pennsylvania State Police.

3. There was no probable cause for the warrantless arrest of the Defendant.

4. Subsequent to his arrest, the Defendant was interrogated by the aforesaid police officers, as a result of which interrogation, the Defendant made

inculpatory statements.

5. The Defendant did not intelligently, knowingly and voluntarily waive his constitional rights in regar' to his interrogation, as a result of the fact that the Defendant at the time of his arrest without probable cause and without warrant and at the time of the initial interrogations, was in a weakened mental and emotional condition and was under the influence of intoxication.

6. All statements given subsequent to the initial interrogation constituted the fruit of the initial illegality in the obtainment of the statements.

7. All statements obtained by the police from the Defendant under the circumstances should not be admitted into evidence because they were obtained in derrogation of the Defendant's rights under the Federal Consti...ion.

WHEREFORE, Defendant prays that a hearing be held upon his allegations and that following such hearing an Order be entered suppressing the use of any and all statements, both oral and written, by the Commonwealth, said statements to be suppressed and not used by the Commonwealth at any trial of the Defendant at the within term and number.

II. APPLICATION TO SUPPRESS PHYSICAL EVIDENCE SEIZED AS THE RESULT OF AN ILLEGAL SEARCH AND SEIZURE

8. After the arrest of the Defendant, the police officers conducted a search of the Defendant's residence aforesaid.

9. Said search was conducted by police officers after said officers had first obtained a search and seizure warrant.

10. The said search and seizure warrant was invalid in that it was not issued upon probable cause supported by a valid affidavit sworn to before the issuing authority.

11. The affidavit submitted to the issuing authority in this case sets forth the aforesaid inculpatory statements of the Defendant obtained in violation of the constituional rights of the Defendant as aforesaid and therefore, the affidavit, search warrant, and subsequent search and seizure constitute the fruit of the original illegality in the obtainment of the aforesaid statements of the Defendant.

12. The aforesaid affidavit also contains heresay statements without setting forth any basis of reliability of said statements.

13. As a result of the said illegal search and seizure made at the residence of the Defendant, police officers seized a kitchen chair, a kitchen floor tile and a blood sample from the leg of the kitchen table, and other items.

14. Police officers also obtained an illegally issued search warrant in order to search a blue Chevrolet Stationwagon bearing Pennsylvania Registration No. 725590S belonging to the Defendant.

15. The search warrant issued for the search of said motor vehicle was invalid in that the supporting affidavit was insufficient for the reason that said supporting affidavit contained alleged statements of the Defendant which were obtained in violation of his constitutional rights as heretofore set forth and therefore constituted the fruit of the original illegality connected with the obtainment of said statements, and in addition thereto, contained heresay state-

ments without setting forth any basis of the reliability of said hearsay statements, and said affidavit otherwise fails to set forth any probable cause for
issuance of a search warrant for search of said motor vehicle.

16. As a result of the aforesaid illegal search of said vehicle,
Defendant believes that the police officers seized items of physical evidence
from said vehicle which the Commonwealth may attempt to use against the
Defendant at the trial of this case.

17. The search of the said motor vehicle was illegal and violative of
the Defendant's constitutional rights under the Fourth Amendment to the U.S.
Constitution, as applicable to the Commonwealth of Pennsylvania under the
Fourteenth Amendment of the U.S. Constitution.

WHEREFORE, the Defendant prays that your Honorable Court order that
the illegally seized evidence and any evidence relative thereto shall be suppressed and not used against him in any criminal proceeding.

III. APPLICATION FOR PSYCHIATRIC EXAMINATION

18. Counsel for the Defendant have interviewed the Defendant, have
studied the records, other memoranda, and data, and believe that the appoint
ment of a psychiatrist is essential to the preparation of the defense in this
case.

19. The preparation of an adequate defense for the Defendant requires
that counsel be accurately apprised as to the nature of the Defendant's mental

health at the time of the crime and at the present time, and be able to consult with and, if necessary, have available at trial a psychiatrist engaged in the Defendant's behalf.

20. The Defendant may offer an insanity defense at trial. Pa. R. Cr. P. 305 C(1b) requires that notice of insanity or mental infirmity defense shall be filed of record at the timre required for filing an Omnibus Pre-Trial Motion under Rule 306. The Defendant will not know of the availability of such insanity defense until after a psychiatric examination. The Defendant therefore requests that the time for filing of notice of insanity or mental infirmity defense be extended until after the completion of a psychiatric examination and after the report of the same is made available to defense counsel.

WHEREFORE, it is respectfully requested that the Court authorize Court appointed counsel to retain a psychiatrist or psychiatrists to examine the Defendant and that the time for filing a notice of insanity or mental infirmity defense be extended until 10 days after the psychiatric report is made available to defense counsel.

John R. Seltzer, Esquire

Dominick Motto, Esquire

-5-

They agreed, and a psychological evaluation was requested.

COMMONWEALTH OF PENNSYLVANIA) IN THE COURT OF COMMON PLEAS OF

vs.) LAWRENCE COUNTY, PENNSYLVANIA

)

FRANK CHARLES IANNARELLI) CRIMINAL DIVISION

) NO. 451 of 1980, Cr.

ORDER

NOW, March 11, 1981, following hearing upon Defendant's Omnibus Pre-Trial Application, it is Ordered and Decreed:

1. Defendant's Application to Suppress statements made by him is refused; and,

2. Defendant's Application to Suppress physical evidence seized as the result of a search and seizure is refused.

BY THE COURT

_______________________ J.

COMMONWEALTH OF PENNSYLVANIA)   IN THE COURT OF COMMON PLEAS OF

VS.   )   LAWRENCE COUNTY, PENNSYLVANIA

FRANK CHARLES IANARELLI   )   CRIMINAL DIVISION

)   NO. 451 OF 1980, Cr.

ORDER

NOW, January 13, 1981, Defense Counsel having requested a PSYCHOLOGICAL EVALUATION of the Defendant, the same is Ordered to be performed by appropriate personnel of the Human Services Center, it being further Ordered that Defense Counsel make the necessary arrangements for all appointments and further advise Human Services Center personnel relative to the nature of the evaluations desired with respect to the Defendant.

BY THE COURT

M. R. Balph   J.

COMMONWEALTH OF PENNSYLVANIA) IN THE COURT OF COMMON PLEAS OF
) LAWRENCE COUNTY, PENNSYLVANIA
VS.)
) CRIMINAL DIVISION
FRANK CHARLES IANNARELLI)
) NO. 451 of 1980, Cr.

ORDER

NOW, March 21, 1981, it appearing that there are pending pre-trial matter in the above captioned case, it is Ordered and Decreed that this case be stricken from the March, 1981 Trial list.

BY THE COURT

_______________________ J.

His psychological evaluation came back.

element of premeditation and specific intent to take life.

The fact that the Defendant acted under a diminished mental capacity sufficient as to negate the element of premeditation is established by the psychological report which was introduced into evidence by stipulation of the parties. The legal concept of negating the inference of a specific intent to kill sufficient for first degree murder through the use of psychiatric evidence has been acknowledged by the case of Commonwealth v. Moore, Pa. 373 A2d 110.. The psychiatric evidence was very similar to the case at bar it is noted, however, that in the Moore case on cross-examination the psychiatrist stated that he did not believe that the Defendant was acting impulsively and it was the facts solicited through the cross-examination of the psychiatrist which diminished its defensive use for the Defendant in the Moore case, However. that is not the situation in this case. In Moore, the court said the following:

"Appellant contends,however, that the psychiatric evidence offered by the defense was sufficient to negate the inference of a specific intent to kill. This testimony, although conceding that appellant was legally sane and not psychotic, did indicate that he was impulsive and had limited control over his emotions and feelings. The finding suggested that appellant experienced difficulty in maintaining a conventional attitude, especially when faced with stressful situations. It was theorized that the victim's threat to contact the police could have presented such a stress situation as to have produced an impulsive response."

-10-

The court in <u>Moore</u> negated the above position of the appellant in that case by pointing to the cross-examination of the psychiatrist in which the psychiatrist undermined his own theory. However this is not the case in the case at bar where all of the circumstances corroborate the psychiatric report and further the psychiatric report fully corroborates the testimony of the Defendant. The <u>Moore</u> case does establish that a psychiatric report along the lines set forth in <u>Moore</u>, that is relating to the Defendant's probable conduct under a stressful situation and his nature to act out impulsively in such situation does negate the concept of specific intent to kill or premeditation necessary for first degree murder. The psychiatric report emphasized the chronic and severe marital discord between the Defendant and the victim, the threat and fear of physical punishment and harrassment from his wife, his separation from his children and the great amount of stress placed upon him by the marital discord and separation from his children coupled with some drinking on the day of the event and the occurrence of a severe argument and the threat of more physical harm from his wife. The report indicates that it would have been the combination of these factors which set the stage for a catastrophic event. The psychiatric report indicates that the Defendant has a low I.Q. between 85 and 95 and that psychological tests reveal a man with an inadequate personality and when under extreme stress the Defendant becomes illogical with an increased tendency to act out. The Defendant is afflicted with an emotional personality disorder of a developmental type and indicates Mr.

-11-

Iannarelli having an increased sensitivity to any physical harm. The report further indicates that the Defendant can be in a disassociated state of mind when he is faced with an overwhelming emotional stress. It is quite conceivable, according to the report, that he could act out, lose control of his behavior, and suffer a state of amnesia. The report further indicates that all of the circumstances combined together could very well have experienced a rage of violence which impaired his judgment, loosened inhibitions, and triggered impulsive action which was then blocked out from conscious memory.

All of the Defendant's testimony corroborated the various factors that the psychiatrist relied upon in making the evaluation that he did make of the Defendant. There was ample evidence of the long history of marital discord which was extremely severe in nature between the Defendant and the victim and much evidence as to the harrassment and punishment inflicted by his wife, including physical as well as emotional punishment, the Defendant's testimony and his demeanor were impressive as to his love for his children and the traumatic emotional stress that he was placed under as a result of having been deprived of his children at various times. There is also ample evidence that the Defendant regularly drank heavily and continued this drinking into the early morning hours of the same morning in which the shooting occurred which further contributed to the diminished state of mind. What is most impressive, however, is the fact that the Defendant does not remember the shooting, he has no conscious recollection of having pulled the trigger. His testimony

-12-

indicates that he went to get the gun in order to calm his wife down, to scare her and to avoid any further physical punishment of himself. However his getting the gun did not have that affect. It made her more angry and caused her to make statements which could have very likely aroused the passion in the Defendant that he had for his children. The victim, prior to the shooting, indicated and said to the Defendant that he would never see his children again, that the children must do what she says or she beats the children and she said that she is the boss. When the victim said the word "boss" all that the Defendant remembers is hearing two noises and then sometime later waking up outside of the house on the ground and then thereafter trying to figure out what happened because he did not know what happened. It is noted in the doctor's report that Mr. Iannarelli's statements throughout the Human Services Center evaluation remains consistent. It is noted that the statements referred to in the report was supplied by testimony by the Defendant on the stand and he again remained consistent throughout his testimony. He was cross-examined rigorously by the District Attorney yet his testimony was unshaken by the cross-examination. As Professor Wigmore states in his treatise on evidence, "Cross-examination is the greatest legal engine ever devised for discerning the truth." It is submitted that if a Defendant's testimony is unshaken by cross-examination and if it is not refuted by other credible evidence then the testimony should stand as given. In the case at bar it is submitted that the evidence of the Defendant establishes that no premeditation was involved thus necessitating a finding that

-13-

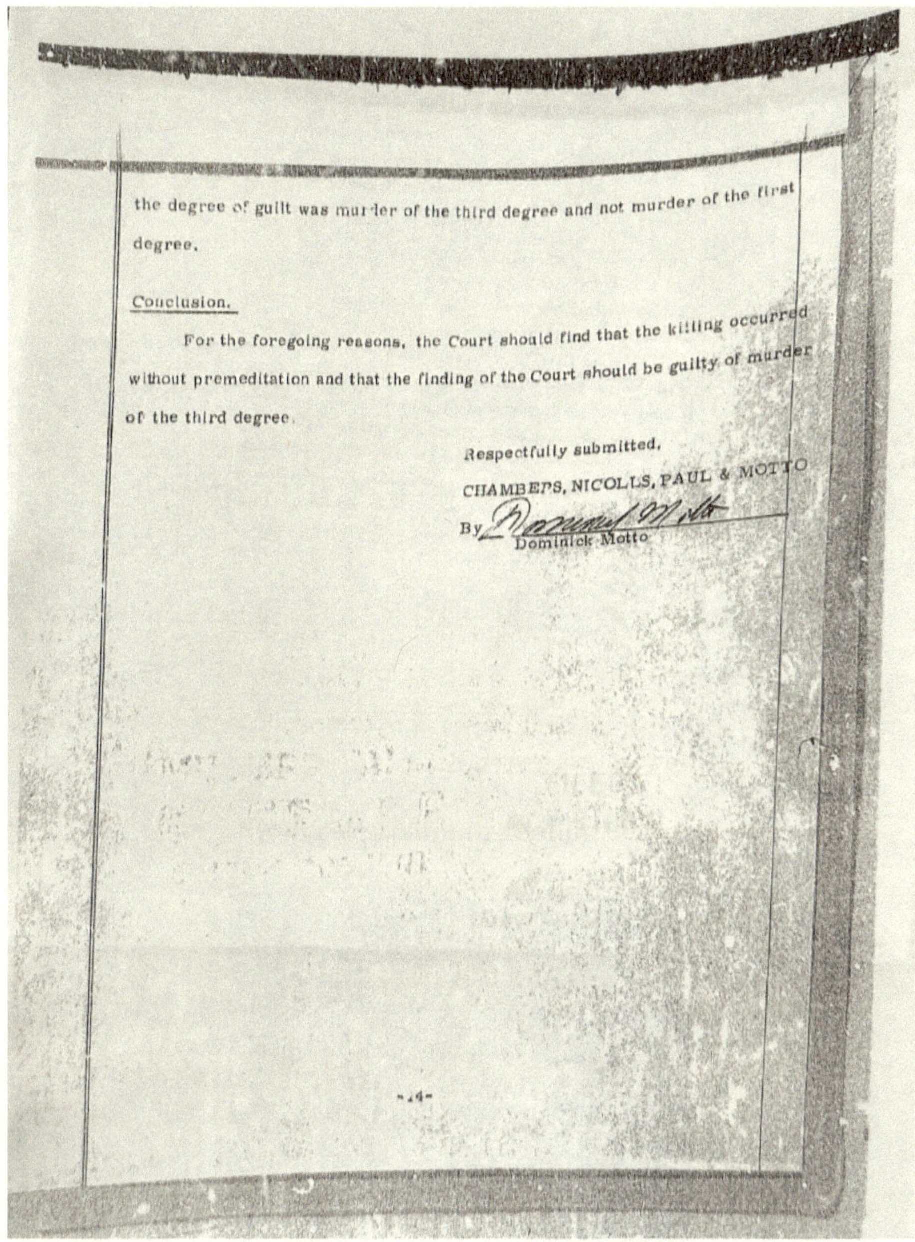

the degree of guilt was murder of the third degree and not murder of the first degree.

Conclusion.

For the foregoing reasons, the Court should find that the killing occurred without premeditation and that the finding of the Court should be guilty of murder of the third degree.

Respectfully submitted,

CHAMBERS, NICOLLS, PAUL & MOTTO

By _________________________
Dominick Motto

-14-

Due to the findings, it was determined that he could enter a plea of insanity.

COMMONWEALTH OF PENNSYLVANIA : IN THE COURT OF COMMON PLEAS
:
V. : LAWRENCE COUNTY, PENNSYLVANIA
:
FRANK CHARLES IANNARELLI : CRIMINAL DIVISION
:
: No. 451 of 1980 Cr.

NOTICE OF INTENTION TO OFFER
AT TRIAL THE DEFENSE OF INSANITY
ON CLAIM OF MENTAL INFIRMITY

Notice is hereby given pursuant to Pa. R.C.P. 305 to the District Attorney of intention to offer at trial in behalf of Defendant the defense of insanity or claim of mental infirmity.

As the result of emotional personality disorder the Defendant had the ability to lose control over his behavior with which disorder the Defendant was affected on August 12, 1980 for a period of which Defendant is uncertain but anticipated to be several hours, and further that Defendant did not meet the minimum requirements of capability set forth in Section 302 of the Crimes Codes (18 P.S. 302) and further Defendant was incapable of understanding the nature and quality of his acts and the difference between right and wrong.

The witnesses other than Defendant that the Defendant intends to call at trial to establish said defense are:

Glenn Moran, M.S./M.S.W.
Human Services Center
P.O. Box 310
13 W. North Street
New Castle, PA 16101

Instead, Dad plead guilty and took a plea deal.

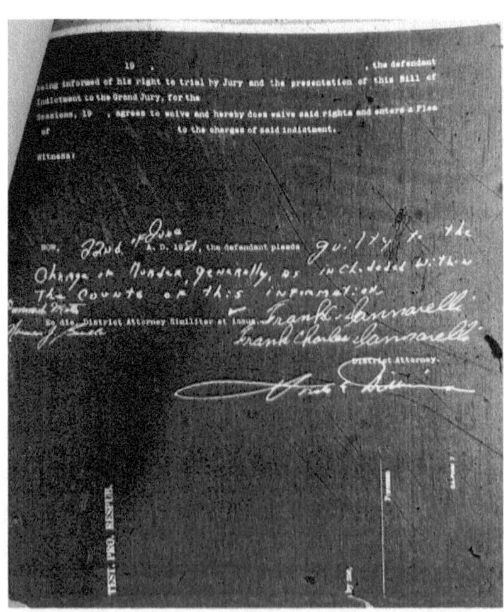

The documents confirmed some of what I had been told. Mom did go to Dad's house by herself. They got into a fight. Dad said Mom hit him with a pan, which was also confirmed in the information I located. He said he didn't remember actually shooting her, that the next thing he remembered was being outside and seeing her buried. It was true that she had been shot three times in the throat, in the kitchen, and that she was buried in a hole by the well. It was true that Dad admitted to it, then took it back, then admitted again. There was no trial. And Mom's van had, in fact, been found at the end of the road.

I also learned new things. Dad had taken a plea deal, which explained why there was no trial. I found out that there had been a Domestic Relations hearing scheduled within weeks of Mom's death. That made me wonder if that had anything to do with why Dad wanted Mom to go to the house in the first place. Had receiving that letter enraged him to the point that he started planning her demise? Is that what sent him over the edge?

JUDGE
J. F. HENDERSON, P. J.

DOMESTIC RELATIONS OFFICER
LUTHER E. SHAFFER
658-2541

ANNEX BUILDING
NEW CASTLE, PA. 16101
July 28, 1980

NOTICE OF CONFERENCE

IN RE: IANNARELLI, Frank and Laura
No. 381 of 1980 D.R.

DEFENDANT MUST BE
PRESENT FOR THE HEARING

Mr. Frank C. Iannarelli
R.D.#1, Box 277
Wampum, Penna.

Dear Sir:

You are requested to appear in the Office of Domestic Relations, Lawrence County Court House, Second Floor, Court House Annex, Court Street, New Castle, Pennsylvania, on ... Thursday, August 21, 1980 ... at ... 2:30 P.M., for a conference concerning the support of your family.

Please bring proof of your monthly income to the hearing for the last six months. Kindly notify your attorney of this hearing, if you so desire.

It is of utmost importance that you be present. OUR OFFICE IS PRESENTLY LOCATED IN THE NEW COURTHOUSE ON COUNTYLINE STREET, NEW CASTLE, PENNA. PLEASE BRING A COPY OF YOUR 1979 INCOME TAX RETURN TO THE HEARING.

DOMESTIC RELATIONS OFFICER

Luther E. Shaffer

LES/bas
cc: Mrs. Laura Iannarelli
cc: Butler, Pa.

I also learned that, toward the end of Dad's prison term, which ironically coincided with the end of his life, he had gone on furloughs, staying with a local pastor for weekends at a time.

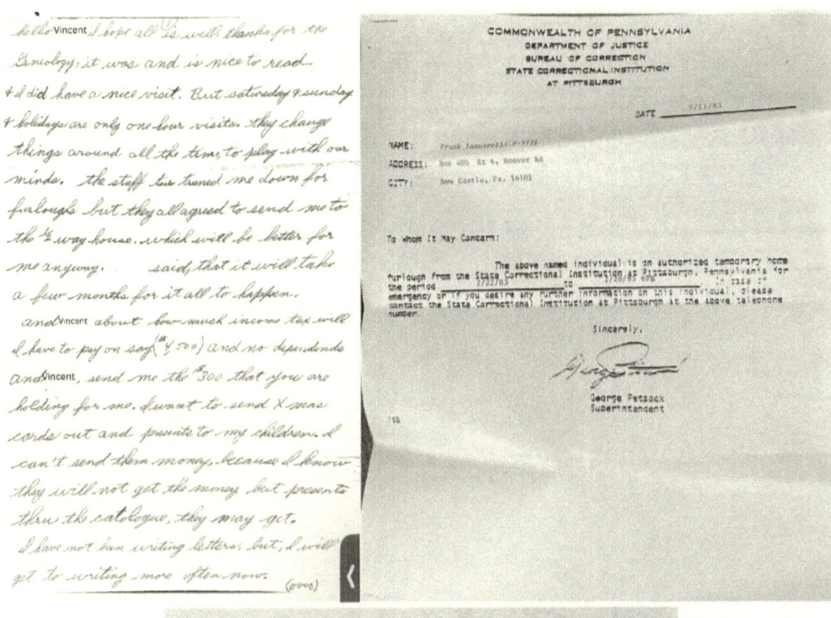

Hello Vincent I hope all is well, thanks for the
Geneology, it was and is nice to read.
& I did have a nice visit. But saturday & sunday
& holidays are only one hour visits. they change
things around all the time, to play with our
minds. the staff has turned me down for
furloughs but they all agreed to send me to
the ½ way house. which will be better for
me anyway.   said, that it will take
a few months for it all to happen.
    and Vincent about how much income tax will
I have to pay on say ($4 500) and no dependends
and Vincent, send me the $300 that you are
holding for me. I want to send X mas
cards out and presents to my children. I
can't send them money, because I know
they will not get the money. but presents
thru the catologue, they may get.
    I have not been writing letters. but, I will
get to writing more often now.   (over)

COMMONWEALTH OF PENNSYLVANIA
DEPARTMENT OF JUSTICE
BUREAU OF CORRECTION
STATE CORRECTIONAL INSTITUTION
AT PITTSBURGH

DATE   9/11/85

NAME: Frank Iannarelli P-5731
ADDRESS: Box 400 Rt 6, Hoover Rd
CITY: New Castle, Pa, 16101

To Whom It May Concern:

        The above named individual is an authorized temporary home furlough from the State Correctional Institution at Pittsburgh, Pennsylvania for the period 2/22/85 to 2/26/85 6PM . In case of emergency or if you desire any further information on this individual, please contact the State Correctional Institution at Pittsburgh at the above telephone number.

                    Sincerely,

                    George Petsock
                    Superintendent

/sb

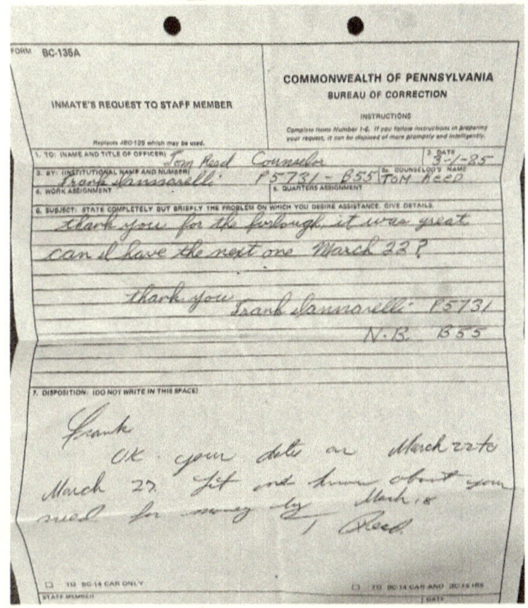

FORM BC-135A

COMMONWEALTH OF PENNSYLVANIA
BUREAU OF CORRECTION

INMATE'S REQUEST TO STAFF MEMBER

INSTRUCTIONS

Complete Items Number 1-6. If you follow instructions in preparing your request, it can be disposed of more promptly and intelligently.

Replaces J80-139 which may be used.

1. TO: (NAME AND TITLE OF OFFICER) Tom Reed Counselor   2. DATE 3-1-85
3. BY: (INSTITUTIONAL NAME AND NUMBER) Frank Iannarelli P5731-B55   3a. COUNSELOR'S NAME TOM REED
4. WORK ASSIGNMENT   5. QUARTERS ASSIGNMENT
6. SUBJECT: STATE COMPLETELY BUT BRIEFLY THE PROBLEM ON WHICH YOU DESIRE ASSISTANCE. GIVE DETAILS.

    thank you for the furlough it was great
can I have the next one March 22?

        thank you
                Frank Iannarelli P5731
                    N.B. B55

7. DISPOSITION: (DO NOT WRITE IN THIS SPACE)

    Frank
        OK. your date on March 22 to
March 27. Let me know about your
need for money by March 18
                    T Reed

I contacted that pastor to talk about my dad. He told me that
Dad was quiet and somber and that he hardly left the house. He said
Dad talked about us kids constantly and that he would just stand in
the living room and stare silently out the bay window.

I pictured him there, looking out that window, lost in thought, and I felt something I never expected; I felt sadness for him. Then I felt guilty. How could I feel bad for a man who had done something so awful? A man who had ruined my life? A man who had murdered my mother? I told myself I shouldn't empathize for him, but I did.

I learned that Dad had moved into a halfway house in Sharon, PA, as a transition to his release. Nobody in the family seemed to know about this, because when I told them, they didn't believe me.

LAW OFFICES
LAMANCUSA & CILLI, P. C.

CARMEN F. LAMANCUSA
GABRIEL P. CILLI
ANTHONY S. PIATEK

302 CENTRAL BUILDING • NEW CASTLE, PENNSYLVANIA 16101
TELEPHONE (412) 658-3728

CHARLES DLUGOKENSKI
(1911 - 1979)

July 20, 1984

Superintendent George Petsock
STATE CORRECTIONAL INSTITUTION
Post Office Box 99901
Pittsburgh, PA 15233

        Re: Frank C. Iannarelli
            Prisoner No. 5731

Dear Superintendent Petsock:

Please be advised that I now represent Frank C. Iannarelli, Prisoner No. 5731, through the Public Defender's Office of Lawrence County. As the records no doubt reflect, Mr. Iannarelli is presently incarcerated at your institution at a sentence for 5 to 15 years; and during the month of August, he will have been incarcerated 4 years of that time.

It is my understanding that Mr. Iannarelli would be eligible for furlough status and placement in a half-way house in Sharon, Pennsylvania, upon completion of 4 years of his 5 year minimum sentence.

Please be advised that I have spoken with the District Attorney's Office of Lawrence County in this regard, as well as the Honorable Judge Francis X. Caiazza; and it appears as though they would have no objection to the same. Judge Caiazza has indicated that should he be sent a request from your institution requesting his possible placement and transfer, he will indicate his desires at that time.

Thus, I trust that you will give Mr. Iannarelli consideration for this program in order that he may avail himself of the promise of employment that exists for him should he be returned to a life without incarceration.

Thanking you for your cooperation and assistance in this matter, I am,

Very truly yours,

GABRIEL P. CILLI

GPC:bal

2-15-85

Frank,

Good news. The Community Services Center (Halfway house) has accepted you. However you are on the waiting list. An acceptance date will be established later.

FORM BC-3C

Transfer Petition

(Replaces BC 2A-3B-4B-44)

COMMONWEALTH OF PENNSYLVANIA
BUREAU OF CORRECTION

IDENTIFICATION OF INMATE

SID NUMBER	BC NUMBER	PBPP NUMBER	NAME
13892539	N-731	8805-D	IANNARELLI, FRANK

COUNTY	COURT	OTN
LAWRENCE	#451, 1980	A674334-3

SENTENCE AND CHARGE	
5 to 15 YEARS	MURDER III

CLASSIFICATION INFORMATION

□ Initial Classification
□ Reclassification

PROGRAM LEVEL: V

REMARKS:

PITTSBURGH CENTER MALL

Accepted Pittsburgh CSC # 2 - April 8, 1985

PURPOSE OF TRANSFER
□ ADMINISTRATIVE
□ SEPARATION
□ YOUTHFUL OFFENDER
□ SECURITY RISK
□ MEDICAL
□ COURT
□ OTHER ___PRE-RELEASE___

Examination of Inmate Completed: Appropriate Classification Information Attached

REQUEST TRANSFER OF INMATE

FROM: SCI PITTSBURGH
TO: PITTSBURGH CENTER MALL

Signature of Official

DATE: Jan 21, '85

TRANSFER ORDER

TRANSFER FROM: SCI Pittsburgh
TRANSFER TO: Pgh CSC

□ Administrative Transfer
□ Temporary Transfer Not To Exceed _____ Days After Approved Date

REMARKS:

Deputy Commissioner For Treatment

DATE: 3-28-85

TRANSFER DOCUMENTATION

Date of Reception	DATE OF PETITION TRANSMITTAL	RECEIVING LOCATION	SIGNATURE AND TITLE

| □ ADMINISTRATIVE TRANSFER | BC-15 (White) | Clerk Of Court (Canary) | PBPP (Pink) | DCT (Goldenrod) | □ TEMPORARY TRANSFER | RIRO (White) | TIRO (Canary) | COR (Pink) | DCT (Goldenrod) |

My sister, Haylee, once told me she had seen someone walking down the street who looked just like Dad. It had startled her. She was afraid. When I suggested that it may have actually been Dad, she told me that it wasn't; there was another man in Sharon who looked just like him. I can't help but wonder if it really was him.

Still, so many questions remained unanswered. Nothing stated why Mom went alone on that day or whether Dad had help. I don't know what was going on inside his head, but I do know that my dad's family is not made up of the monsters that I was told it was. I have become quite close with many of them in my adult life, and they have been nothing but kind, supportive, and loving toward me.

I also know that my mom was loved. Both my mom's family and my dad's family have told me stories about her: how she would sing while she walked around the house and that she was, in fact, always singing. That she was smart, a go-getter, always trying something new. How she had opened a pizza shop in West Pittsburg, an hour north of Pittsburgh, and called it *Laura's Pizza.*

They say it was the <u>best</u> pizza.

I've been told stories about my dad too. That he was a functioning alcoholic, went to work every day, came home, ate dinner with the family, and then went to the bar. I was told that when he wasn't drinking, he was a nice guy, that everyone loved him. That he even sang at people's weddings. But the drinking…

For the longest time, I thought he was only abusive when he was drunk, but I recently learned that that wasn't true. I learned that he could be happy one minute and raging mad the next. That one time he had beaten my mom with a board while she stood in the creek behind our house, and another time he came after her with a knife, and she pushed him, causing him to fall on it and stab himself in the forehead.

I don't know if that's true, I never know what is actually true. I have a picture of him from prison, and I don't see a scar.

Dad

Honestly, it was easier when I thought he was only mean when he drank. With that understanding I could blame the alcohol and not the man.

CHAPTER TWENTY-NINE

LIFE BEFORE DEATH

Sometimes I close my eyes and try to feel myself in the presence of my mother; her smell, her smile, her voice, her laugh. I reach for her in my mind, but it's like chasing shadows in a dark room; she's always just out of reach. The fact is, I barely remember anything about my mother at all. It saddens me, it frustrates me, that I cannot recall her. I long for my memories so much that I can't even put it into words. I've been told over and over again that I should be thankful that I don't remember being little, living with Mom and Dad, because it was such an awful existence, that there was constant fighting, constant turmoil. Of course, that's easy for people who aren't the ones who can't remember to say.

Here is what I do know, or at least what I think I know anyway.

Mom grew up and lived with her family in the same town where Dad lived, West Pittsburg, Pennsylvania. She was young when she met Dad; Dad was actually 21 years older than Mom. Mom was working for my dad's brother, Uncle Vincent, when they met. Mom got pregnant with her oldest, Haylee, and gave birth to her when she was 18. Mom and Dad got married at some point. I don't know if it was before or after Haylee was born, but I think it was before. I'm told that they eloped.

Mom

Throughout their marriage, they had four kids, as I previously mentioned: Haylee, Brian, Lisa, and then me. I think I must've been a surprise because Haylee, Brian, and Lisa were all born around one year apart from each other; then, five years later, I was born. Also, I'm told that Mom had her tubes tied and that she had one of her ovaries removed after Lisa was born; I guess I'm definitely supposed to be here.

For some reason, Mom and Dad expected me to be a boy. They were planning on naming me Larry. Surprise, it's a girl. They didn't have a name picked out, so they decided to name me after my mom. I love this. I didn't grow up being called Laura, though; they called me LuLu. Apparently, Dad started calling me Lu and then Louie. Mom didn't like me being called that and quickly started calling me LuLu. The name stuck. To this day, some people still call me LuLu or just Lu.

Mom was kind, smart, caring, and, as I previously mentioned, always trying to make something of herself. She had a pizza shop. Later on, she had another pizza shop. At one point, she had a store out of our house. She was always trying something new. I'm like Mom in these ways; I'm a go-getter just like she was.

I remember that we had chickens. I've been told stories of how Mom would cut the chickens' heads off, pluck their feathers, and prepare them for dinner.

I remember that there was a giant hill behind our house and that sometimes we would try to climb it. That was just us kids, though, not Mom. I don't know if I ever made it to the top or not, or if any of us did; I don't think I did.

I've been told that Mom and Dad fought often, mostly after Dad came home drunk from the bar. Sometimes Mom would hold me because she knew that Dad would leave her alone if I was in her arms; I was his princess and he wouldn't hurt me. I've been told that Mom frequently carried around the bruises from the abuse she endured from Dad. I've been told that shortly before Mom took us kids and left, Dad had beaten her with a 2x4 in the creek out back; that she decided that was the final straw, that she needed to leave if she wanted to save her own life. I've been told that when Mom and Dad started fighting, we kids would often run downstairs screaming and crying, begging them to stop, and that sometimes we would run over to the neighbors and ask to use their phone so we could call for help, but that help stopped coming because it happened so frequently.

This is something that resonates within me, and that is also heartbreaking to me, especially knowing what the outcome ended up being. I imagine being in that moment as the child making the call, waiting and waiting for help to arrive, and feeling abandoned by the world when it never did. How did we return to the house then, knowing what we had just witnessed, knowing that nobody was coming to help us, and knowing that we were walking right back into what we had run across the street to escape? As an outsider watching this happen repeatedly, though, how does one decide where to draw the line?

When I was four years old, Mom left Dad and took us with her. I was sad to be leaving with Mom. Like I said before, I never wanted to be with Mom; I always wanted to be with Dad. Mom had rules that I had to follow, and Dad let me do whatever I wanted. I vaguely remember sitting in the bed of our truck, I think we had a cap on it, while Mom drove away. I remember trying to talk to Brian, who was sitting in the front seat with Mom.

We kids, Haylee, Brian, Lisa, and I, all knew sign language. It's funny that at such a young age that that is something we all knew. Only the letters, but it gave us the ability to communicate with each other when we couldn't speak, like through the back window of the truck. I found out as an adult that there was a man who worked as a bartender at the bar where Dad would take us; he is actually the one who taught us sign language.

When Mom left Dad, she moved us to Alabama. We stayed with Mom's cousins for a little while. I don't remember any of that.

We then moved into a trailer park, and then to another trailer park. I vaguely remember that we moved into an apartment complex at some point. I remember that Haylee would watch us while Mom was at work. One time we decided to make cookies, but we didn't have all of the ingredients, so we went around borrowing them from our neighbors. I remember another time Haylee took a drink of spoiled milk and ran around the complex gagging.

Mom then bought a piece of property in Alabama. We didn't have a house or anything on the property, so we lived on the property in the back of our truck; five of us. The truck had a camper that covered the bed of it, and that is where we lived. Mom would take us to a nearby gas station so we could get cleaned up.

Mom met Joe while we lived in Alabama, the Joe that I previously mentioned as her fiancé. At some point we, Mom, Joe, Haylee, Brian, Lisa, and I, all left Alabama and moved to Texas. After about a year in Texas, we moved back to Pennsylvania, about a half hour away from Dad's house.

I always thought that if Mom hadn't moved back to Pennsylvania, maybe the tragedy that ended her life wouldn't have happened. Maybe us being so close to Dad, yet so far away from him, added to his inability to handle the situation. Not that she was rubbing it in his face, but maybe she was, or maybe he took it like she was. Of course, there are always "what ifs."

I have only one memory of my mom. We were driving on a road that runs behind West Pittsburg, past the power plant. There was a tower of some sort that stood high above the power plant; it had flashing lights on the top of it. I remember asking Mom why that tower was there and why there were blinking lights on top of it. She told me that it was so that nobody would hit it. My young mind at the time had more questions because why would they build something and put lights on it just so it wouldn't get hit? That didn't make any sense.

I have two memories of my dad.

I remember him driving us kids home on the road that our house was on. I was sitting on his lap while he drove with one knee. It was like I was driving the car.

The second memory I have of Dad includes our dog, Bullet. He was our white German Shepherd that I mentioned earlier. He was always chained up by his dog box outside. One day, I was home with Brian and Lisa when Bullet's chain broke. I remember him running around, dragging his chain. I remember being afraid because he forced his way into the house through the front door. The door was at the bottom of the steps that led upstairs. I started running up the steps with Lisa, terrified. Brian closed the door on the chain so Bullet couldn't come into the house the whole way. Brian then called Dad to come home and take care of it. Dad was only five minutes away, at the bar. Dad was always at the bar. Lisa and I sat down on the steps and waited while Brian tried to calm Bullet down. I don't remember anything else about it. I suppose this memory is more about the absence of Dad.

These small moments are all that I remember of Dad. I thought he was fun and that he protected me; that's how I saw him anyway. I mean, I was only seven when Mom died, and the fighting and turmoil and such was the life I had always known, so to me, that way of thinking made sense.

The memories I have of my mother and father are so fragmented, incomplete, and fleeting. I try to piece them together, but there are so many missing pieces that it feels impossible to form a complete picture. When I think about those memories, though, I wonder how much of my perception is real and how much is the product of a child's mind trying to make sense of a confusing and chaotic situation.

CHAPTER THIRTY

THE SEARCH FOR MEMORIES OF MOM

As I previously stated, I remember very little about Mom. I went on a quest to find out as much information as I could about her and to find as many pictures of her as I could.

Mom's fiancé

I decided I wanted to get in touch with Joe, my mom's fiancé. Honestly, I don't remember him either. I had heard about him, nothing good, but nonetheless, I wanted to find him because I thought for sure he would have some stories to tell and some pictures to share.

Realize that I was searching for him back before we had all of the technological advancements that we have today. I was able to use the internet, but it was difficult, to say the least. My main place to look was through online phone directories, so the search was slow. At first, I couldn't find anything on him. As it turned out, I had been searching for him under the wrong name, a quest that felt as elusive as finding information about her. I learned that Joe wasn't actually his name; that's how little I knew about the man who had loved my mother. His name was George, but everyone called him Joe. Once I learned his true identity, I began my search again from the beginning.

I ended up finding part of a family tree somehow that one of his sons had put on the internet. Through that, I got in touch with one of his daughters, Phoebe.

When I was little, Phoebe and I were the best of friends, inseparable, from what I'm told. Unfortunately, I don't remember her from my childhood either. I was, however, so happy to get to talk with her. She provided me with enough information to use to lead me to her father. I found a phone number to what I believed was his house, and I called it.

A woman answered, Shirley, George's, Joe's, wife. I introduced myself, twice actually, as she didn't understand who I was or why I was calling. Once we got past the shock of the introduction, she was very sweet and kind. She told me that Joe was a truck driver and that he wasn't home. We talked to each other for almost an hour. She told me that he had told her stories about my mom but that she was never sure if the stories he told her were true or not because she never saw any articles or anything about it. Then she told me something that melted my heart. She said, "Joe never got over the loss of Laura. Joe loved Laura with all his heart. Since she died, he has never loved anybody the way that he loved her." It made me smile to know that she was loved in such a deep way, whether he was a good man or not.

Shirley then told me that she and Joe were in the process of getting a divorce. She gave me the number to where I could reach him, at the truck yard where he was working.

I was filled with hope as I prepared to make the call. I was excited to have the ability to speak with him, and I expected him to be happy to hear from me. I took a deep breath, and I called the number. It went to voicemail; I hung up. I wasn't prepared to leave a message. What would I even say? I paused, then I pulled myself together, and I called back. When the answering machine came on, I left a message: "This message is for Joe. This is Laura Iannarelli. Please call me back," and I left my number. Now I realized then how shocking of a message that must have been for him to hear. After all, I am named after my mother; her name was also Laura Iannarelli. There wasn't really any other way I could say it, though, for him to know who I was and for me to get a return call, so I went with it.

Shortly after I left the message, he called me back. He was surprised to hear from me and eager to talk. He told me how much he missed my mom. I asked him for pictures; he said he had some that he would send to me, but he never did. He asked about each person in my family, by name, to see how they were doing. He told me that he drives his truck to Youngstown, Ohio sometimes and that he would get in touch with me when he would be in the area so we could meet up, as Youngstown wasn't too far away from my house. I was so excited at the idea of meeting him and talking about Mom. Nobody ever talked about her with me. He gave me his direct number and said that he was definitely going to keep my number. I was so happy to connect with him. I felt like I was finally going to learn more about my mother. I looked forward to seeing him and taking in every story he could tell me. I called his number a few months later, since I hadn't heard from him and hadn't received the pictures he said he would send, but the number had been disconnected. I was dumbfounded. I didn't see that one coming. By that point, though, I was so used to people leaving me abruptly that this was just another chapter of my life that closed too soon. I didn't even bother with trying to find him again; he had my information and could get in touch with me if he wanted to. To this day, I've never heard back from him.

Pictures from Aunt Johnie

I was reaching out to everyone I could get in touch with, trying to find pictures of Mom. I called my Aunt Johnie; she was my grandpap's sister. She said that she had pictures of Mom and Dad from their wedding day and invited me over to see them. I couldn't wait. I planned a day and went to her house. She prepared a nice dinner to share with us and told me stories about Mom and Dad. She said that they fought a lot, but that it couldn't have all been bad; after all, they did have four kids together. I froze for a minute when I heard those words. How could she be so cavalier about the situation? Surely she wasn't excusing the physical abuse that had been inflicted upon my mother. After all, Mom did eventually leave the abusive situation and then was ultimately killed at the hands of it. I didn't confront her about her comment; I did, however, develop an instant disdain for her, and I guarded myself in that gathering moving forward. When it came time to see the pictures of their wedding, she said that she actually didn't have any. I was dumbstruck. Why on earth would she say she had pictures when she knew all along that she didn't? Did she not understand the quest I was on to find memorabilia of Mom, to find answers? How could she be so ignorant, to flat out lie to me about such a delicate topic? I never spoke to her again.

It was after that that I found out that Mom and Dad had eloped and that nobody had pictures of their wedding because the pictures didn't exist.

Tapes of Mom singing

From what I'm told, Mom spent a lot of time with her sister, Shirley, my Aunt Shirley. One thing they liked to do together was record themselves singing all kinds of songs. I remember her singing one of the songs: "The Hearse Song." Ironic.

I think I remember hearing these tapes being played at some point, though I don't know when I would have ever heard them. When I imagine myself hearing them, I picture Mom and Aunt Shirley sitting on the left side of the couch in the living room that was in the house that I lived in with Mom and Dad. I picture Mom's dark hair; she's wearing her glasses, and Aunt Shirley is sitting up against her. Mom is holding a little microphone that is attached to the tape recorder, and they are singing. Maybe I am actually remembering them recording the tapes, or maybe I made this image up in my mind; I don't know. What I do know is that my Aunt Shirley has the tapes, or had the tapes. My sister and I have asked, begged, her repeatedly to let us hear them. I would love to hear Mom's voice again. I don't remember it at all, so that would be breathtaking. Also, maybe hearing her voice would trigger other memories. Maybe she laughs on the tapes; I would love to hear her laugh. Aunt Shirley states that she doesn't know where they are, though, that they may have been destroyed when her home was damaged, by fire, I think. I don't think she would lie to me about it, but I don't think the tapes are lost either. In a strange way, I'm hoping that I will find out someday that she was just too afraid to give them up, to lose that piece of her sister that she treasures and hangs on to. Someone once told me that they can't imagine that Aunt Shirley doesn't know where they are, as she always kept them right beside her on the end table next to her chair.

The scrapbook

Through a conversation with my sister, Haylee, I found out that Mom had created a family scrapbook and that Grandpap had it. She said it had pictures of all of us kids in it. I couldn't believe that such a treasure existed. I lit up when I heard this. Finally, something I could look at from Mom. Maybe there were pictures of Mom in it. I needed to get my hands on that scrapbook.

Haylee said that Grandpap attempted to give the scrapbook to her at Mom's funeral, but she told him to keep it because it held such sentimental value. I couldn't understand why she wouldn't want that for herself, for us. I asked her about it, and she said that she did want it but that she felt that it was the only piece of Mom that Grandpap had left; that he looked so broken at the funeral, so she offered that piece to him. That was very kind of Haylee, to put Grandpap's feelings before her own during such a traumatic time for all of us.

So, there we were, years later, having this conversation. Grandpap had already died, and nobody had ever mentioned the scrapbook. I decided I needed to locate Grandpap's wife or their son to see if they had it. But how on earth was I supposed to find them? Nobody ever talked about them. I always felt that they were not accepted into the family, since she was the wife that took Grandma's place.

As I previously mentioned, Grandpap was married to Sharon. Together they had a son named Mark. I had heard that before Grandpap died they lived in Arizona, where Grandpap owned a landscaping business. I was also told that since Grandpap's death, Sharon had remarried, but nobody knew what her new last name was, except maybe Aunt Johnie, and I couldn't ask her. This wasn't much to go on back then, but I was determined. I searched the on-line phone books in Arizona for "Sharon Smith"; needless to say, that was a pretty common name. I called several of them. I spoke with many Sharons who were all very nice but who were not the Sharon I was looking for.

I needed a new plan, so I started calling all of the Mark Smiths I could find. No luck there either. Next up, I called landscaping companies in Arizona. I asked them if they knew my Grandpap, as he used to have a landscaping company; I was hoping that maybe Mark had taken over the family business and I would find him that way. All of my efforts were for nothing, and I was feeling quite defeated. So, as my final-ditch attempt, I hired a private detective. I gave him all of the information I had and hoped for the best. To my delight, it only took him a couple of days. He called me to tell me he had found Mark. I couldn't believe it. After the long search, Mark and I were connected.

We were happy to talk to each other. We briefly shared stories with each other in regard to how our lives were going, about people in the family, and about how much we both miss Grandpap. Then I asked him about the scrapbook. He had never seen it or even heard about it. He asked his mom, Grandpap's wife Sharon, but she didn't know anything about it either. I was so sad to hear this; my heart just sank with disappointment. After not even knowing the scrapbook existed, to spending months searching for Sharon and Mark, to hiring a private detective, to now find out it's not something they even knew about and didn't have was crushing. Who knows what could have happened to it. Maybe it got lost when Grandpap moved the family to Arizona. I had no idea. I figured that was the end of that.

I dwelled on the loss of that scrapbook. It made me feel frustrated and so sad; how could something that held so much sentiment be lost or even worse, forgotten? I was upset that it wasn't located. I was even upset with Haylee for letting Grandpap keep it in the first place, as if it was her fault that nobody knew about it or where it was. Still, I couldn't understand why she wouldn't want to hold on to that precious treasure. After all, I had to blame someone.

A few months later, to my complete surprise, Mark called me. He said that he was clearing out the bottom of a china cabinet for his mom when he saw something stuffed in between a bunch of papers. He pulled it out, and lo and behold, there was the scrapbook! I could not believe it. I cannot even accurately express in words how completely shocked and delighted I was that he found it. Things never turned out this way for me. Since he lived on the other side of the country, it seemed like it took forever for it to arrive via mail. I eagerly waited and excitedly checked the mail every day.

I had no idea what to expect of this scrapbook, what would be in it, or missing from it. I imagined pictures of us on family vacations, holiday get-togethers, pictures of Mom playing with us in the yard. I couldn't wait.

The day finally came; it was in the mailbox. I called Haylee so she could come over and we could look at it together. The front page read "Our Photo Album Frank and Laura Iannarelli Dec, 1973." I was taken back for a moment when I first saw the cover because Mom had signed it. My signature looks exactly like hers, not just because it's the same name; the slant and everything are identical. Incredible.

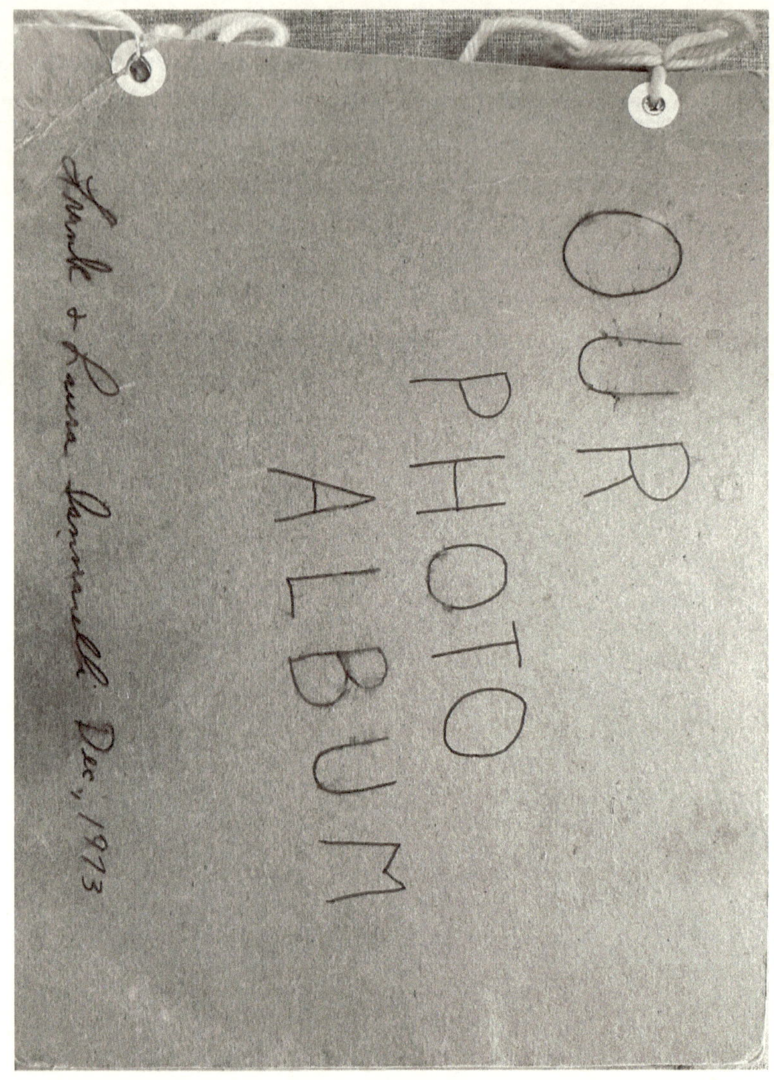

So many emotions came over me as I held that scrapbook. I couldn't open it fast enough! There were pictures of all four of us kids together: Haylee, Brian, Lisa, and me. I was just a baby in them, and I was happy to see all of us together and that we looked like we were taken care of.

Brian, Haylee, Lisa, and me (the baby)

Most of the pictures were, of course, of Haylee, Brian, and Lisa because they were older. I mean, I was born the year the scrapbook was made.

I felt a bit of strangeness when I saw the big, beautiful smiles on the faces of my brother and sisters. How were they smiling so big? Was there a time when everyone was as happy as the pictures portrayed? Did I miss it? I hadn't ever heard a story about a time when our lives were not filled with turmoil and violence. The lies in the smiles on their faces made me want to scream because it made me realize the walls they had presumably built up so young to hide the sadness and fear that was behind them.

I was disappointed to find that there weren't any pictures of Mom in the scrapbook, as that is what I was mostly searching for. There was one picture of me being held up by Dad's hands. This is sweet for me; it's actually the only picture I have of me and Dad together.

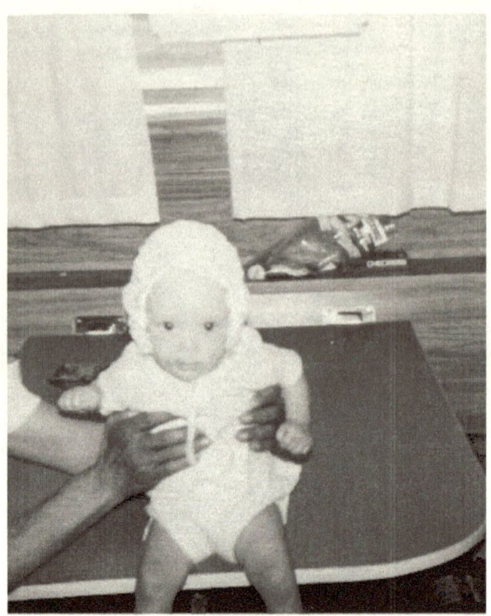

Dad holding me up

There were also pictures of my older brothers and sisters, our grandparents (dad's parents), and several other extended family members and friends. There was one large picture of Dad with all of the kids from his first marriage, but Dad was torn out of it. One day one of my siblings was looking through the scrapbook and came across this picture. He asked in disbelief why anybody would tear Dad out of the picture! We all just kind of looked sideways at each other because it was obvious to us why that would happen. I mean, the scrapbook was with my grandpap; my mom's father. There was no way he would want a picture of Dad in his home. It would've been nice to have that picture intact, though; I mean, he's still our dad.

What a true treasure this scrapbook is to have.

The Necklaces

Haylee gave me two necklaces that belonged to Mom. One has a larger oval shaped piece dangling from the chain that can hold two pictures.

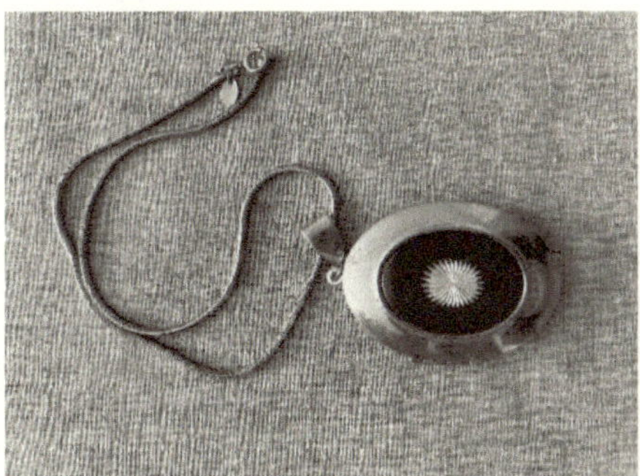 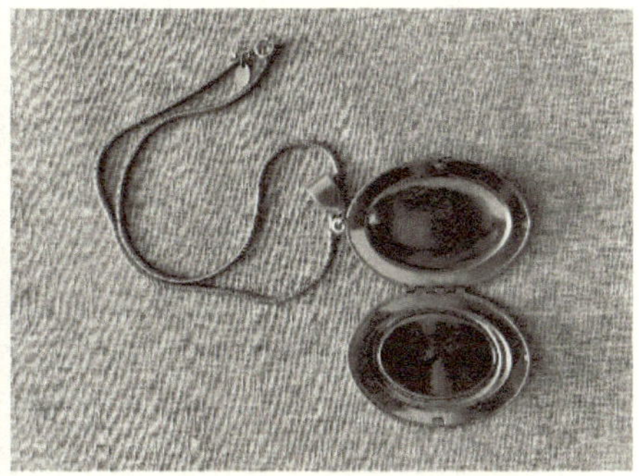

The other one is smaller with an antique look, and it is beautiful! It has a larger center with places for three pearls surrounding it. Two of the pearls were missing, but it didn't matter. I cherish that necklace, even to this day. I make a point to wear the necklace whenever I feel like I might need some extra encouragement, when I'm having a bad day, and on special occasions. I know it's silly, but it makes me feel like in some ways Mom is close to me on those days. One day, years later, Maria surprised me and had the two missing pearls replaced. What a kind and thoughtful act that was. It was so heartwarming. Now it's even more beautiful than it was before. I love having that necklace, that small piece of my mom that I get to carry around with me.

I have one picture of me with Mom. I am a baby in the picture, and Mom is holding me on her lap. I have the picture hanging on my wall. This picture is very dear to me.

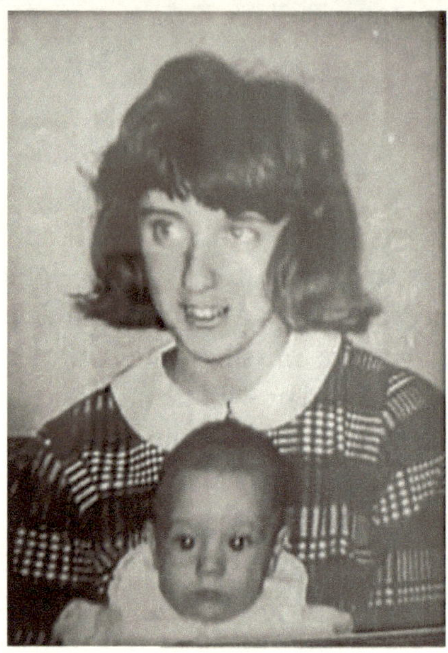

Mom and I

I may never have all of the answers, but the pieces I have found gave me back something else. My mother's voice, my father's shadow, and the strength to keep searching.

CHAPTER THIRTY-ONE

AS A MOTHER

Becoming a mother was something that I always wanted more than anything, something that I had longed for. I wanted the family, the connection, the unconditional love that I imagined should be automatic in a family. I wanted to give that to my children, and to feel it in return.

I knew I could be a better mother than what had been modeled for me by my aunt. I knew that I would give my child(ren) unconditional love, that I would support them, that I would do everything I could for them. As their mother, my children would never question their worth, their purpose, or whether or not they were loved.

As I previously stated though, I never thought it would happen for me; that I would actually become a parent. The dream of being loved by a man who would want to have a family with me seemed so unreachable, almost laughable, so much that I had convinced myself that that piece of it would never happen, not to mention the idea of me being physically able to have children. When it did, I was taken back, and ecstatic, and it was never something I took lightly.

Although I knew the kind of mother I longed to be, I always feared that the negative ways in which I had been raised were too ingrained in me to change. That terrified me.

I remember one day when I lived with Aunt Judith that I was outside sled riding with my cousins; I wanted her to be out there too, sled riding with us; but she wouldn't come out. I couldn't understand why she wouldn't want to play with us. I asked myself what she could possibly be doing that was more important. I remember thinking that I wanted to be the kind of mom who played with my kids; that I never wanted them to feel like they were not important. Honestly that's something I've always struggled with though; knowing how to play with them. I've always been there for them, but playing with them has never come naturally to me.

I learned in one of my psychology classes that the child who rebels the most from their parent or parental figure is typically the one who ends up being the most like the one they rebelled against. I was confident that I never wanted to parent the way that Aunt Judith did, but learning this made me afraid that I would be just like her. As a parent, I made, and still make, a conscious effort to check my own actions so that I can be certain I was/am not parenting like she did. I have noticed situations as a parent that reminded me of Aunt Judith's approach. When this happened, I immediately stopped dead in my tracks, imagined the situation as if I was hovering over it and watching it take place as a whole, and then I changed my approach.

My youngest daughter loves horses. She plays with horses, rides horses, and sometimes even pretends to be a horse. The other day she asked me to go outside with her to 'play horse'. I was right in the middle of cleaning up the messy house and deciding what to prepare for dinner so I could actually cook it, plus I was tired. I didn't want to stop what I was doing to go outside and play, so I said no. I instantly saw the enthusiastic radiance drain from her face. It was as if I had taken away all of her joy. It was heartbreaking. I realized in that moment that I had done to her what I said I would never do; I made her feel like she wasn't important; like she was less important than everything else. I was overcome by the disappointment she was feeling, as I felt it too. I regrouped, put on my shoes, and went right outside to join her. As it turns out, I'm excellent at cantering.

Haylee has told me on a few different occasions that my parenting style is like Mom's. My calmness, my connection with the kids, and the way I guide them and try to understand them are all things that are similar. I find that intriguing since I don't actually remember anything at all about being parented by Mom. I take it as a compliment though; a compliment that reassures me that Mom is in me somewhere. It makes me smile to know that I am like her in some ways.

When I became a mother, it marked the start of my new life; my new identity, if you will. My self-esteem was still low, but it was improving, and as a mom, I was no longer without purpose; my children were my purpose. Every goal I set, every choice I contemplated, every decision I made, was with them in mind. Now, it might not seem like that was the case, as I've made an incredible number of wrong moves along the way, but, it's true. I mean, I never claimed I was good at it.

As I previously mentioned, Maria and Patrick were born to my first husband, Patrick Sr. Vincent and I had two more children: Vincent IV was born when Maria was seven and Patrick Jr. was six; and Isabella was born two years after Vincent IV. I didn't know I could feel as much love as I felt/feel for each of these children. Each time I was expecting the next child, I would wonder how I could possibly share the love I felt for the child(ren) I already had with another child. The funny thing is, I didn't have to share it; my love grew to include each new child! When Isabella was ten years old, we adopted a beautiful baby girl, Ivy. What a perfect family. I overflow with love and adoration when I think of each child that I have been blessed with.

Remember, I didn't have a positive mother figure to guide me along my way, and I had experienced a tremendous amount of trauma in my childhood that, although I tried to overcome, was still deep seated within me. The struggle to overcome it was daily. I was emotionally growing myself while I was molding these precious lives that were entrusted to me.

For guidance, I found myself, unintentionally of course, attaching to other people's mothers; my friends' mothers, even the mother of my older siblings. When I look back at the times I pushed myself into situations with my dad's first wife, when I was standing right beside her in pictures at gatherings, it makes me cringe! It really wasn't my place. The members of my family were very kind about this though; they never said a word.

Spending extra time with these mothers, watching their moves, imprinting on them, became an unconscious regular part of my life. I never really asked a lot of questions of them; instead, I observed their techniques and learned what I could from them that way.

Some of my friends' lives seemed so perfect, so together. I envied the closeness they shared with their mothers, the grown-up conversation they engaged in, the family photos that were hanging on their walls, and the get-togethers they had regularly. I wondered how they did it; how they maintained their calmness and level-headedness; how they developed and maintained good relationships where they were happy to see each other and happy to spend time together, where there didn't appear to be manipulation or ridiculing involved. I wanted that, all of it. I strived to build a family life like theirs. I couldn't wait to have a family picture hanging on my wall!

I started looking more deeply at myself. I analyzed everything I did, everything they did. I read self-help books, I read books of others who had overcome childhood suffering and the loss of their mothers, I joined motivational groups online (when that became an option). I imitated positive qualities I saw in people I perceived as accomplished. I went to church. All of this was helpful. Most importantly perhaps though, was I remembered what I felt like growing up. If I made a move that in any way resembled my own negative childhood experiences, I stopped, looked at the situation, and moved in a different direction.

Disciplining my children was something that was hard for me. I was used to being beaten, degraded, and ridiculed as punishment. I didn't want that for my children. I'm not saying they never got a spanking, but that wasn't my go-to, and it wasn't anything like what I had experienced as a child. I wanted my approach to come from love, not anger; from a place of guidance to stimulate positive change, not to instill fear and submission. I wanted to be the person the kids came to, not the one they ran from.

There were times when I would be furiously frustrated with the kids; when they weren't listening to me, when they were defiant, when they were arguing with me; whatever the case; where I would have no idea what to do and I would be so mad that I would want to beat them, like not in a teaching way, like in a way that would mirror what I had grown up with. In those moments, I would stop myself and I would remove myself from the situation altogether. When I was married to Vincent, I would tag him in to take over. We made a good team in that way.

Like I said, this wasn't easy, to change what I had experienced, what I knew; to identify new techniques, to implement new strategies; but I knew I had to break the cycle, and I was determined to do just that. I said it before and I'll say it again; the abuse ended with me.

As I previously mentioned, I have five children. Four of them are grown and have moved out of the house. My youngest is ten and of course still lives at home. Each one of my kids is unique in their own way, and they are all extraordinary individuals; I don't use that word lightly. They are kind and caring to others, they see the positives in people, and they are determined to reach goals that they set for themselves. They are always there for each other; they truly have each other's backs, no matter what the personal sacrifice may be. I feel that they get all of that from me. They are a true reflection of the effort I put into breaking the abusive cycle. Sometimes I wonder how I got so lucky to have a houseful of kids who are kind, caring, hard workers, and beautiful; each and every one of them. Maybe it was ingrained in me, and was passed down from Mom.

CHAPTER THIRTY-TWO

LETTERS FROM DAD

I hesitated to add this chapter, these letters, to this book, because doing so gives Dad a voice. A voice to say anything he wants about Mom without her having the ability to refute any of it. I don't have letters from Mom, so she doesn't have that same voice.

In these letters, Dad blames Mom for causing him to murder her. What?? He expresses this numerous times through his written "apologies." His way of thinking is troublesome at best. He is responsible for his own actions, plain and simple. He made a choice to end her life and carried it out. He told people numerous times that he was going to kill her. He bought a gun. He took the gun out when they were arguing. He waved the gun around. He killed her.

He claims that he was protecting us kids and that his hands were tied. I'm not sure about any of that. He claims that he was beaten by her and that he was afraid of her. I suppose she probably did try to fight back, but I know that she's the one who walked around with bruises from his frequent beatings, who would stay out late at night with us kids in hopes that he would be in bed sleeping before she got home, and who was on edge every night when she expected him home from the bar because she didn't know if he would come in and go straight to bed or if he would start a physical fight with her. He claims that she took his kids away. We know that is true, in an effort to save her own life and maybe even ours. He claims that she committed adultery. I found out that yes, that is true. He claims that she beat us kids. I don't remember that happening, but I don't *remember anything from before she was murdered aside from the few things I've mentioned elsewhere in this book.*

I want you, my readers, *to know that just because I decided to include these letters, that does not mean it's been determined that what he wrote depicts an accurate account of the reality. Perhaps his words are true, perhaps they are partially true, or perhaps they are his way of seeing things through his own-colored glasses. I suppose I will never know. They say there are three sides to every story: his side, her side, and the truth.*

I made the decision to include this chapter because I want my readers to have as much information as I have to make the story as complete as possible. Including these letters does not mean I agree with or support the murder of my mother, and it does not mean I believe everything that is written.

Furthermore, you will notice that some of the names have been removed from these letters. I did that to protect the identity of those whose names were written. Where I could, I replaced the empty spaces with the names I have used throughout this book.

As an adult, I was given a big brown folder that I was told had letters from Dad in it, letters he wrote while he was in prison. This was exciting to me, and completely unexpected. I had no idea something like this even existed. After all of the searching I had done, to have letters from Dad seemed unbelievable. As I held that folder, I experienced a strong wave of emotions: anticipation, worry, and even discontentment. What was in it?

I pictured the outside of the house where we lived. The kitchen where Mom was killed. I pictured our dog, Bullet, on television running around, carrying the heavy weight of his chain. I always found the weight of that chain symbolic of the weight we all carried when we lived there, whether we knew it or not. I pictured the overgrown gravesite where I've had to go to visit my mother, and the nicely manicured gravesite where I've visited Dad.

I was filled with a mixture of resentment, apprehension, and desirousness. It was like I was having an internal struggle with my feelings. Should I be happy that I have these letters or concerned about what might be in them? I thought maybe these letters would give me more of the answers I had been looking for. One thing I knew is that I couldn't wait to read them.

As I read them for the first time, I hung onto every word, searching for answers.

Dad's early letters refer to him getting his affairs in order.

Hi, [Vincent]. How is everyone and everything? Did you get your trailer shoved yet? [Vincent], I need a pair of reading glasses. my arms are too short now, and the words are blurry. I can't make them out. Do I need an eye examination first or can you just get me a pair of reading glasses? I think they sell reading glasses and they don't cost much.

Is there a statement from the bank this month? I figure there should be one and there should be a bank balance in the checking acc. bring the statement in

2

and I can get a check from [Attorney] to pay you for the glasses. And [Vincent], don't give the [Smith's] no more information than you already have. Tell them to see [Attorney] [Smith's attorney] is only using you as a friend. Let the [Smith's] pay [their attorney] for his time and work. don't give him no more information. all the [Smith's] keep Laura kid from me. at this time. So the hell with them. I can't see the trust fund

3

they are talking to you about. they would take money from the kids instead of giving them any. They only want the kids for what they can get. Security, that's all. [Vincent], I don't want you to worry about this but when they took me to the hospital, it wasn't for my back. I had sharp pains under my left shoulder blade. I was doubled over and short winded. The pains were sharp and they hurt. I couldn't stand up. these men layed me down in bed. the pains were with me for a

4

while, when they carried me to the bed in the hall way, that is when the pain went away. they took x-rays of my left side and my chest. and they took the electric heart test. and after the Doctor read them all. he said that my heart is real good. all the test they took was for my heart. This Doctor here is setting up an apointment to have me examined to find out why my left arm and hand and fingers are dead. My left arm has been dead on me for at least 3 weeks. at times I can # raise it. but I have no control over it. from the elbow down it shakes. I have no

5

feeling in my left arm or fingers. I don't want you to worry about it. I'll be O.K. and I feel certain that the judge will post bond on me, and let me go to work. at first, it will leave the kids where they are, untill I know what is what. [Vincent], I will never get drunk again. I miss drinking at all. I know the biggest mistake I made was, I should have taken my problem to the priest, instead of the bottle of beer.

I am alone in here. I can't talk to these men. all they talk about is crime, and jail. It is

6

all they know. They spent all their life in jail. They leave jail and within a week, they are back in. I keep to myself mostly. I eat with them, we talk about the food. at yard time, We go outside. they play basket ball. I walk around the yard. and talk to the guards. we go out in th afternoon from about 2 to 4 P.M. Everyone is good to me. The guards all like me. you know they let [Vincent] I'll visit for 35 min last night. this morning I was thinking how happy the kids are now. their letters now are happy ones now.

7

and I thought of their letters of when they were away from here. And I cried. I was on my knees at my bed for a long time crying and praying and thanking God that the kids are happy and in good homes and being well cared for. I get these feelings time and again. I'm allright now. I'll write again later Joe. Bye for now.

Frank

1

Hello [Leonardo and Jane].
How are you? I know you and Uncle [Vincent] call each other that is good. Is [Lisa] giving you and [problems?] I don't think so, she is very loveable.
I have been waiting to hear from you. I don't know why you don't write. I guess you are busy. I heard you had [Brian] playing baeball, that is good, keep him in sports.
I don't know when my trule will be. But I am sure, I will be set free. how did it go with mister and [Smith] [Haylee] there? I think he is a honest man. It is the

2

[Smith] women that we can't trust. [Leonardo] and [Jane] write and let me know how everything is going. I am thankfull that the kids are happy and at last now. I know where they are and I can write to them. and they can write to me. tell [Jason] to write to me.
I'll write again later. Bye for now.
God Bless all of you.
Dad

4

4. [Vincent] it was nice talking to you. I am sending a check. as I need any money I'll ask you. all I want to say is, if something should happen to me then, ~~what~~ give the money to [Leonardo] for the children. what I mean is don't give the state none. the sherrif never did give me a report of the sherrif sale. the hell with the state.
I will write more later when they bring my glassis to me. If you write, send me Room. Motto Phone No.

5

I'll write more later,
Frank

hello [Vincent]. Buy me a <u>black & white 9"</u> TV at a store like sears. they have to ship it here. <u>8"</u> will be fine. you pick it out. I believe a TV in my room will help a lot. thank you, you know, something to watch. to help keep my mind clear. no bigger than 9" my room is a real small room.
bro. Frank

    I talked to Frank Sr. on the phone on Tuesday nite. He is OK, and pleased that the kids are doing fine. He knows the phone call is off, until the kids are completely adjusted to living in Michigan, and are able to cope with the happenings of 8-12-80.

        Love,
        Uncle Vincent

1

Hello Leonardo and Jane

    I pray everyone is fine. I am proud of you. I heard that Mr. Smith wants to meet the kids. That if you will set it up that he visits one at a time. I like it Leonardo. I love it. He sounds like he is of a grandfather. I think we can trust him. He want to know that they are happy. But don't trust none of the Smith women, Leonardo as you know, I don't have no income in here. All I have is what people leave me. So I can't send you any money for support of the children Leonardo. I have no

2

hospital coverage for the children while I am in here. I can't keep it up with no income. I don't know what to tell you.

    Maybe you and Ricardo & Toby can cover them on your policies while they are there with you. They should have some coverage.

    My attorney has talked to the judge about letting me get on bond. The judge told him to hold off for another couple of weeks. Everything that my attorney has told me, it sounds favorable that he will post bond on me.

    I will send the children spending money as I can. And I will tell

3

them to share it. Unless you tell me not to send them any. I don't want to cause no problems. At home I gave them an allowance each week. They handled their money well. They shared it up and bought things they really needed. Like you, that they wouldn't ask for. I was real pleased how they handled their money, for their young age. I thought it was wonderful. I feel certain Leonardo that God will tell the judge to release me on bond until the trail. I do alot of praying to God I always did say my prayers. And I am

4

sure that he forgives me. But I know I am being punished. The children are happy and they are well cared for. And the letters I get from them now are happy letters. Their letters of before made me cry, they blew my mind. I will tell you when I see you. And I feel sure that it will be soon. I wrote my girl Haylee a letter, and she didn't answer. I can't find out for sure who she is living with. I wrote sent the letter to her aunt Judith address. Weather Judith gave it to Haylee or not I don't know. Uncle Vincent is trying to

5

find out where Haylee is but the Smith's will not tell him. They are keeping her from me. It will take time, but we will find her.

    I'll write to me, when I learn anything new I will let you know.

    God bless you, and I love and thank you for all you are doing for us. Bye for now.

        Dad

1 — 10-16-80

Hi Vincent,
It was nice seeing you and talking to you. You were right about [Attorney]. He was here to see me and told me to quit funding the case because I don't have the money to pay him. But I would be better off, because the court will appoint an attorney and the county will pay him. O, & I guess I got a readjustered

2

letter from an attorney today and they are for [Consumer Co.] & if I don't pay them in full in 35 days they will sheriff sale the property. I have been thinking about it, and I guess just let them sell it. The hell with [Smith's Attorney] and the [Smith's] pay their attorney. Let the [Smith's] all the debters have a lean

3

against the dead. Don't they? Let the court and the attorneys fight it out. You have enough of your own work to get done. Any trust fund with the [Smith's] as trustee, the kids would never get a dime of it. I got my check book now. I gave [Attorney] a check for $250. He promised to work with the new attorney. Joe, I want you with help.

4

to take the stove, it is pretty new, upper oven and lower oven. Take all the tools out of the cellar, there are tools in the hall closet too. the lawn mower and garden tools. You'll find a place to keep all these things. Give the beds to who can use them. Maybe someone can use the dressers too. take the tape player and the tapes, all the books from the front room. Oh two speakers on the player. [Lisa] wants the big Holy Bible.

5

By law, the house & property is laura's, so let her have it. If and when I come home. I will rent a place and start over. [Work] said my job is waiting for me when I can go back. I will be free of all debts. and I will have more to offer and give the kids. all I can say is

6

the hell with the property [Smith's attorney] should know now that the [Smith's] are lyers they told him we are divorced, and we were still married. but don't tell him nothing. when he finds out how they really are at the trail. then that will be in my favor too. Mom and Dad's trunk is up stairs. I

7

want you to take it and keep it. I want that to be keep in the family.
I'll write again.
[Frank]
Get all this done as soon as possible. I am sure [Paul] will help you and his son.

There were letters to and from us kids, well, none from me, but Haylee, Brian, and Lisa had written and received letters.

When he was first imprisoned, he truly believed he was going to be released on bond prior to his trial.

Hello [Leonardo and Jane],

I am happy to know that everyone is fine, and happy. [Leonardo] I can only make long distance Phone Call between 9 AM to 4 P.M. Monday thru Friday. So all I can say is to let me know a day Monday thru Friday that the children are not in school. They do get days of now and then. But let me know in advance. Then I can set it up. Thank you very much.

My attorney is petitioning the court to post bond on me. He feels positive that he can

2

get me out on bond. It won't have to be cash it will be property. Under this bond, I can go home, go to work, and bring the kids home, and we can be together and be happy. My neighbor [Blanche] will come down and cook for us. [Leonardo], I know that Uncle [Vincent] and my nephew [Vincent] + [Albert] will do what they can for property bond for me. You talk to your brothers and [sister] and let me know how much bond I can count on from all of you. [Leonardo]

3

this property bond will let me out, and cover me until my trail. There is alot in my favor, that I can not tell you now. But, [Leonardo] please, you all get together and tell me. I am asking you as your Father. There is no risk, nothing for you to worry about. I haven't had a drink since I been in here. and the truth is, I don't miss it. That was just a bad habit. I promised God in my prayers all the time that I will never get drunk again. And I wount never again.

4

I will write again, you answer and let me know one way or the other. From the mail I get from friends, I don't think I'll have any trouble getting bond set up. Hope to see you soon.

Dad

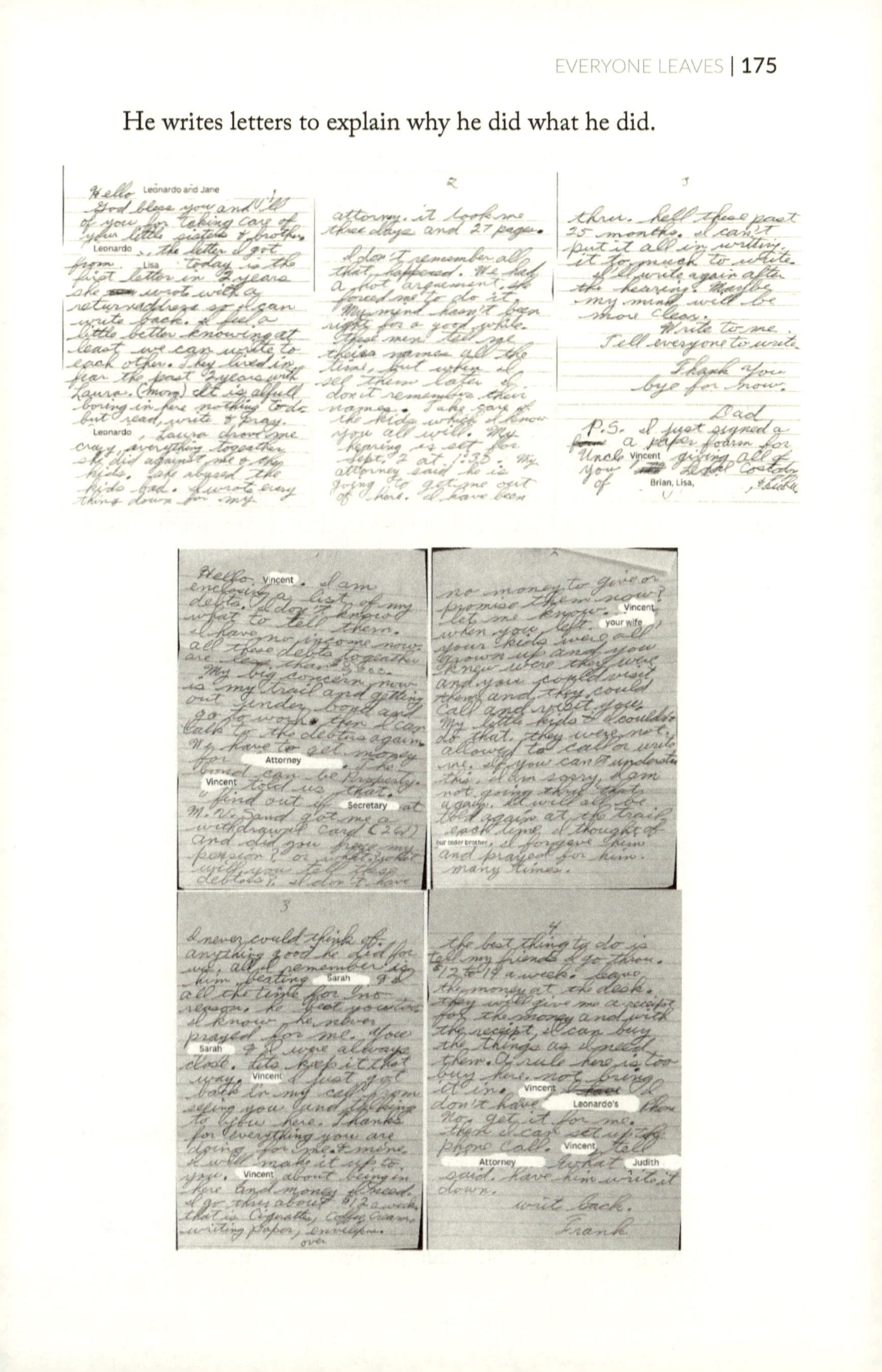

He writes letters to explain why he did what he did.

There was a letter from Dad that was written to Brian and Lisa. He talked about me in it and said how he would sing *Joanie, Please Don't Cry*, and I would cry. As I was reading it, I paused so I could listen to the song *Joanie, Please Don't Cry*. I don't remember it, but I found myself trying to picture Dad singing it with us. It made me smile to visualize happy memories from my childhood.

I wish I had the letter that Dad had written to me, the one that Aunt Judith took away from me back in fourth grade. From what I'm seeing in the letters he wrote to everyone else, I imagine it probably said similar things: that we would be together again and that I was safe now. Little did he know the type of situation I was actually living in. Afterall, I was living with Aunt Judith by the time I received that letter from him. I know he wasn't happy about that, but he didn't know what I was dealing with in that environment. Still, I wish I had the letter that was written just to me. I would love to be able to read his words, written for me alone.

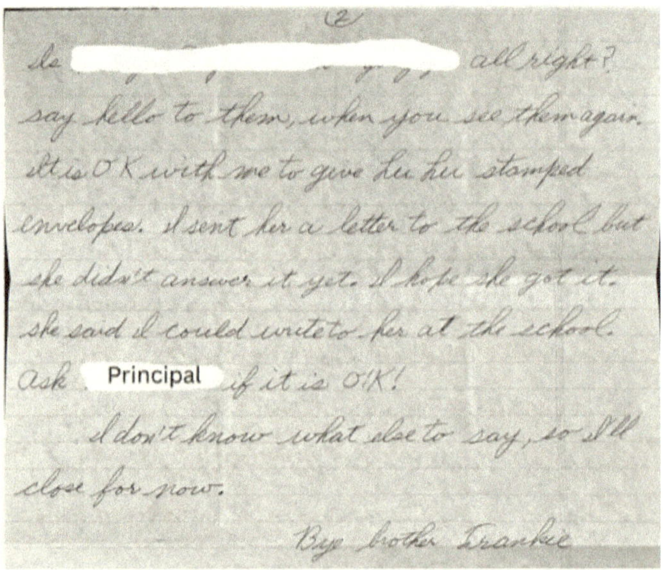

Through his letters, Dad says he was protecting us. I've come to believe that he truly thought he was. That in his mind, he thought we would be better off without Mom. I was told once or twice that before Mom died, Dad said he wasn't going to lose his family again. He had been married before, they divorced, and his family moved out of state. I believe he couldn't bear living knowing that a similar situation had happened in his life again, all the while ignoring the fact that he was the common factor that had pushed them away.

In his letters, he repeatedly refers to us not having to live in fear of Mom anymore, saying that we didn't have to be afraid.

I have come to believe that he had the whole scenario planned out. With Mom out of the picture, he would have his family back. He says repeatedly that he missed us kids and wanted us to be with him. He says in several of his letters that "The Smiths," Mom's side of the family, were no good. He says that he was praying for us. He said that "his people" would take care of us. I stopped when I read that. Who were his people? I really would like to know the answer to that question, especially since none of them ever showed up for me.

There's a part of me that wants to believe him, to think his actions were misguided love rather than pure destruction. But what if he wasn't protecting us at all? What if this story I cling to is just a way to make his actions bearable? If I let that go, what am I left with?

The main things he talked about through his letters were us kids, finances, and the Smiths. As I read them, it seemed to me that he was desperately trying to get his point across about why he committed this deadly act, as if he wanted everyone to be on his side. He also seemed frustrated that the attorneys weren't able to get him out of prison quickly. It was important to him that he kept in touch with us kids and that we understood, though that is a strong word, why he killed our mother.

He said that during a phone call with us kids while he was in prison, we told him that we forgave him. As I read this, I thought: What? No way. We were young, traumatized, learning to navigate our new existence, and didn't even know what we were talking about. Our mother was gone. No doubt we still loved our dad even though we knew he was the one who killed her. After all, that is the only life we had ever known. But we had no way of knowing anything different than what we were faced with, let alone the lifelong impact his actions would have on our lives, our relationships, and our ability to trust others. I think it's a stretch to believe that after a month and a half, we had forgiven him. It makes me wonder, was his mind so distorted that he really believed we did?

As I read his letters, I thought of the time frame when they would have been written. I was so young. The grown-ups had to make all of the decisions for me. That had to be a terrible position for them to be in. I think of my older siblings, the ones who took us in at first: Leonardo, Ricardo, and Sophia, and how difficult all of that must have been for them. After all, they had lost their father too. Sure, their experience was substantially different from mine, but I can only imagine that they were dealing with a certain level of grief themselves. On top of that, they had to make decisions for us. Life-altering decisions.

In the letters Dad sent to Leonardo, he was practically begging him to take us to the prison to see him and to arrange phone calls for us to talk to him. I guess there was a phone call arranged at least once, because Dad refers to it in one of his letters, but I don't remember it.

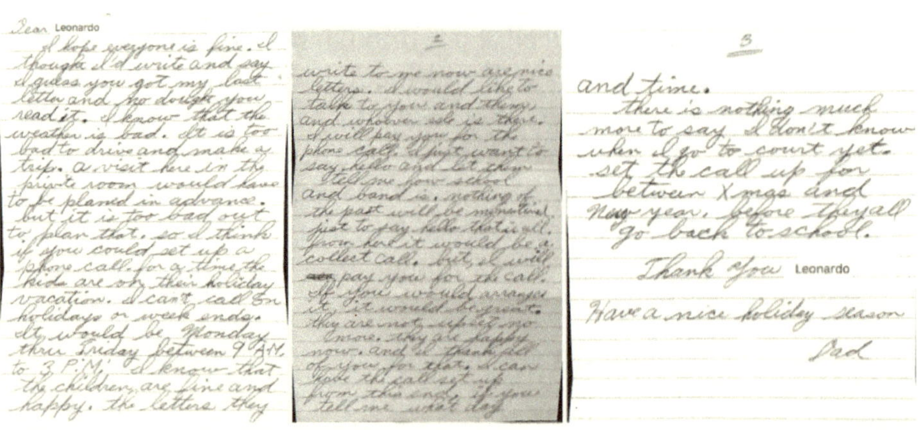

Hello Leonardo and Jane

I have to write and tell you that this morning when I got up. (Sunday) I felt pretty well. All them pains I had in my head, that traveled around my head, were all gone and, I didn't have them all day. I thank you for th phone call. And I know by the children's voices that they are happy and contented. It was the first phone conversation in over 2 years that we talked and they said all they wanted to say and they didn't cry. I thank God all the time for blessing all of you. That same day I talked to you. I had a private visit with brother Vincent and his son Vincent for one hour and that hour really went fast. So that was a busy and happy day for me. ____, I know that I drank to much, I didn't miss any work from drinking. All the problems I had and I didn't get no help from my attorney or none of the law offices. I drank more. But I promised God that if and when I can go home that I will never get drunk again. And I woun't go to the bar no more, and that is a promise that I will keep. ____ James Father of the Holy Cross church come to visit me. I told him that I did not want to prove in court all that Laura was gluity of. The holy commandments she broke the neglet and abuse to the children, everything. Father Siler listened, and he told me to let my attorney know how I feel and to take my attorney's advice and maybe it woun't be nessasay to prove it all. I told him to that I don't care to prove it to man and ___ women. Father Siler agreed with how I felt. I will take his advise.

When Diana sends me pictures of all the children remind her to write down their names and Birthdat. As I have money, I want to send all them a birthday card. A lot of my friends have been droping some of here for me. I don't much here. As I can I want to send them cards and children will like that. And I want to do what I can. If there is any information or what ever, that I can help with. I will. Jane, I am sorry I didn't get to talk to you. I would have liked to. I don't know what else to say now. Tell everyone Happy New Year. I am enclosing some money. God bless you for all you are doing.

Dad

I do know that I never went to see Dad. I wanted to see him. I don't know what I wanted to come from a visit with him; I just know that I've always been upset that I never saw him again.

Like I said, though, that had to have been an impossible decision for my older siblings to make for me while I was with them. I know without a doubt that they were only doing what they thought was best for us, and I would never fault them for that. In fact, I am grateful that they even took us in at all. Aunt Judith, on the other hand, wouldn't even talk about Dad. I suppose she had her own struggles that she was dealing with that didn't allow her to take my needs or feelings into consideration, but she was the adult, so that's no excuse.

One thing that stood out to me as I read his letters, which I feel is important to note, is that Dad does not apologize for killing Mom, not once. He said he was sorry in one letter, but it seemed that he was sorry that he was not with us kids, not that he had taken Mom from us. I was told once that Dad had grown to hate Mom and Mom's family. He goes on to acknowledge that his drinking was a problem, but then blames others for its intensity.

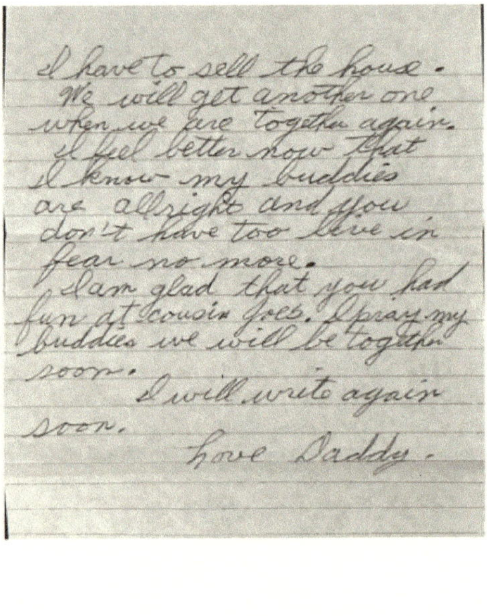

How could he have never felt remorse for what he did, and more so, for killing another person, his wife, the mother of his children, a person that he once claimed to love.

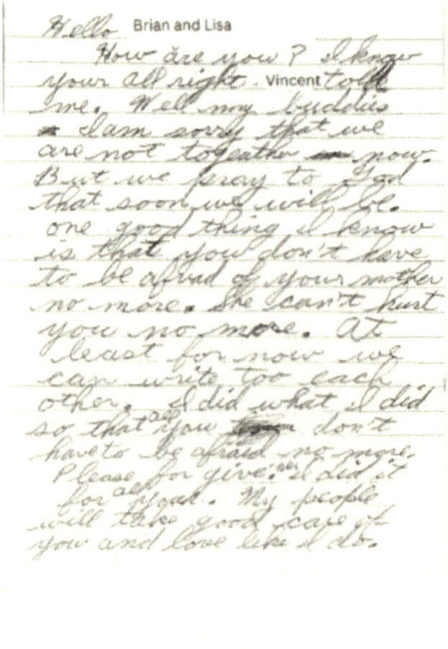

1

Hi [Vincent] I wrote [Brian] a letter like you told me to. I know he will understand, I told [Ricardo] & [Karen] when they give the letter to [Brian] to be near him, in case he wants to ask them any questions. [Attorney] and I are to be in Court on 10-14-[40] at 9:30 A.M. for Arraignment. The Judge is going to talk to [Attorney] next week after this trail is over that is in Court now. He will talk about my bond. Joe is certain

2

he will set a bond on me. I'll let you know how it goes when we get out of Court on the 14th. I hope I get out and go back to work and I will haft to take things one step at a time. I know I will go and visit the kids soon as I can. Did you find out [Haylee's] address? let me know. Give thanks to who did my cholths. I'll have cholths out this Sat. morning too. This doctor is making arrangements to send me to the hospital for a complete Exam. to find out what

3

is wrong with my left arm. Find out the Cause, why the arm is dead and why it shakes. Thank God there is no pain. I have no strenth in my fingers at all. Say hello to everyone for me. I will write again soon.

Frank

1

Hello. Leonardo and Jane

Leonardo, in answer to your letter. With Laura, my hands were tied. I loved her very much and I trusted her, as a husband should. What she did was all for herself. She robbed and stole me blind. she was never a mother to the children, she was never with them. she was mean and crule to the kids. They were scared of her. she beat them.

I couldn't divorce her, because the sherrif couldn't ~~find~~ serve the papers on her. since June 21ˢᵗ of 78 she didn't live at the address given. she was runing and hiding. and her family kept her hide. and under cover. I had no communication with her or the kids. She married me for security and that is why

2

she wanted the kids. Laura is guilty of adultry, stealing from her husband and children, forging may name on my checks. when her resturant in Bessemer went out of buseness. she left here, took our 74 pickup truck and the kids and went to Grand Bay ala. June 21-78 for 5 full months I didn't know where they were. She lived with her uncle. she did get a job there. how many ten times I prayed and cried for the kids. she sold my truck in ala. she signed my name to my Compension check to go there. We had a $2000 loan against the truck. She stuck me with an $8,000 loan in Ellwood City. against the property. In stead of getting a job and

3

making these payments, like
she promised. she just ran
away from her bills. I
found out the hard way that
her and her people don't
believe in paying their bills.
She left Ala. in March of this
year. From March till June she
traveled so much, she had
the kids, Haylee and Lu Lu,
in 3 different schools. Texas,
here in Mt. Jackson and
Slipery Rock. She was still
running from Bills she left
behind. Brian and Lisa was
with me at that time. Lisa
went with her mother in
May and was sick again of
her. In May, June, July Laura
was living within 2 miles
of home and Brian and I
couldn't find her.
the kids and I have been

4

than hell on earth. In May I
got over a $200 phone bill.
Long distance calls Laura made
from different states down south
to her sisters in wampum and
calls to Portewille, All over.
when she took the kids to a
phone to talk to me. back in
the end of 78 and 79 they
were so upset and homesick
for me, that they cried on
the phone. It is just to much
to talk about on paper. I
went there brought the kids
home in 79 the only cloths they
had was what they had on.
no glasses, no games, no
nothing it made me sick.
The kids asked me to take them
home and they didn't want me
to stay and visit. "Please take
us home to Penna." So we
went home.

<u>5</u>

I spent time with them, and
gave them what children need.
A father's love and attention. One
time when I took them to the
play ground and played with them.
"Lu Lu, told. Lisa & Brian
"I am going to marry dady,
when I grow up and old
enough." We told bed time
stories, we sang songs
togeather and we acted the
songs out. Ask them to
sing 'Don't cry Joanie) and
Lu Lu will cry.
Leonardo, I remember back
when you were with me.
I took you and _ _ and
your team to little league
games. _ was a
coach. _ couldn't make
it as a pitcher. But you
and _ played. I took
you to Cleveland stadium,

6

and enterdudused you to Chuck Tanner manager of the Chico White Sox. at that time. I guess you don't remember. Leonardo I came to Michigan to bring youse home on vacation but when I got there, Betty changed her mind and youse weren't aloud to come. But I did get to visit all of yous. I knew that all of you were well cared for. Betty was a good mother and she is a good grandmother. I paid support to her for youse. Leonardo I can't talk about what happened the morning of Laura's death. By your letter, you think you are a judge. I am glad you will not be on the Jury. I prayed many times to God that no

I

one in the world ever goes thru what the kids and I did. The sheriff and other law offices are witness for me because I had gone to them for help. That morning everything came to a head. She came to the house mad. we got in a hot arguement she hit me on the head with a heavy frying pan. the pan put a whole in the wall. I was sitting at the table. I went and got the gun (a 22 pistol) I tried to clame her down. She was wild. she stood there at the sink, her hand in the knife drawer. And she said "when I take the girls back to day, you will never see them again, the girls do as I tell them or I beat them, I am the boss."

8

when she said boss the gun went off. I remember hearing two nouses. the next I remember we were out side, she was covered from her knees up. All I covered was from her knees down. she was liveing with other men and charging what she could to me. I had two back fuseions Leonardo, & they are alfull painfull. Laura caused me to have my 2nd fuseion. June of 77 we had an arguement, I was walking away and she beat me in the back with her fist. Leonardo in here all these things cross my mind and at times I cry. And I will tell you this. In Sept. they had to take me to the hospital for sharpe pains I had in my left shoulder

9

blade. I had a stroke. since then I have pains in my head. they are little pains that travel around my head. most of the time they starte on the left side of my head and travel around the forehead, to the right side of my head. my left arm is dead. there is no feeling in it. no strenth at all. when I raise my left arm to the highth of my shoulder, it shakes out of controle. I thought that I could tell you all, now that I know how you all feel about me. It won't bother you all.

For the long Xmas vacation from school. what I need is to see My little children. The Warden will let us have a visit in the visiting

<u>10</u>

room. with the distance you have to travel, he will let us visit for a coupl hours. After the kids see me. it will be easier for them to understand that they can't be with me. and living there will be better on their minds. But if you don't want them to see me. Then it will be on your mind. You didn't arrange a phone call. It will be up to you now. Ask God if he allows the children to love and visit their Father.

I am sending some money to ~~he~~ get everyone something for Xmas. I know it isn't much, but it will help. Maybe you can put something in all the children's stockings. God knows I am

VI

sorry... Leonardo, I need to see
the children while I am
living. I can't talk to them
after I ~~and~~ am dead.
It took awhile to write this
all down, I think of letters
... Lisa and Haylee ~~to~~ sent
me and they still tear me
up. I am sorry for parts
of this letter but I
am tore up. I was worth
at least $50,000. I had
all my children in mind
to leave it all to. all 8
of you but, Laura said
it is all hers.
All The bills I was stuck with
counting everything & taxes t
heat amounted to $1,000 a
month. My attorney and the
Judge is having me examined
by a doctor to ~~de~~ ~~se~~ determine
I was out of my mind

amd crazy. If you and your brother can find it in your heart to arrange a visit. God will bless you.

Dad,

P.S.
I love all of you, and at night as always I pray for God to bless all of you.

Merry Christmas and a Happy New Year to all

God Bless you.

Dad.

As time got closer to Dad's release, he was making plans to get all of us back together. He couldn't find Brian and Lisa.

Hello Vincent (1) 4-15-84

I'm sending you this deposit slip, you can deposit the money in my savings account. like we said. when I am done reading all about the money market information. I will get back to you. And I don't want all this money on my acc. hoi anyway. it was nice seeing you and Freddy; it took them one full week to send that check to you, I'll tell you all about it on our next visit. Joe, find out if Brian and Lisa are living in Porterville, their card and letters come back to me, so I can't write no more to them.

(2)

well, that is all for now, I got to get a letter off to Mrs. Cowher. I owe her one for a long time. I hope she isn't upset with me. she is a great and wonderfull women. Bye now

Frankie

3-6-87

hello, Vincent I got your letter. good to know that ___ is doing well, and he is home. I was called in friday morning (3-4) about the furloughs and pre-release but they turned me down for now. I asked why - and they said they would vote on it again in august and I would get it then, they want me to be closer to my minimum than just ½. but I know, it fits right in with how they play with our minds all the time. they find ways of turning everyone down the 1st time. so I was expecting to be refused. they did tell me to keep doing as well as I have been and in august I would get pre-release, so now I have to wait it out. and Vincent when you answer send me the address to First Seneca Bank. I have the card you sent me. I'll fill out the card and have my signature notarized, here and I will open a (over)

savings account (2) in the bank in new Castle. my Social Security Card is in my wallet there, at your house. if I need the S.S. card, then you can send it to me too, along with the bank address. And too, Vincent can you get me an F.B.I. address to write to about my children. I do not want to invoke my counselor you know, I did get one letter from Lee Dee mailed from youngstown Ohio. or should I write to Ann Landers? I think I should write to the F.B.I. who is

Lawrence C BA
108 S. South St.
New Castle Pa. 16101

And what does C BA stand for?.

well I hope you can get me all this information. thank you

Bye now

Bro. Frank

I didn't really get any answers from his letters, only more questions. Dad admitted to what he had done. As I previously stated, he said numerous times in the letters that he did this to protect us kids. What was he protecting us from? I never heard anything negative about my mom that we would have needed protection from. Then again, people just may not be sharing negative things about Mom with me out of respect, due to the situation. Who knows? One thing I can say for sure is that I was glad I had the opportunity to read his words, even if they are distorted.

CHAPTER THIRTY-THREE

WHEN WE STOPPED BEING 'WE'

As an independent adult, I felt that I had overcome the trauma that I had endured as a child and that I was emotionally healthier, better able to make friends. They say once you leave high school your life changes, that you meet new people, form new friendships, and gain your independence. I never thought much about this; after all, I was just trying to survive it. I was really looking forward to that stage in my life, though, where I would meet these new people. It turned out that becoming a house parent at the residential treatment facility put me in a situation where this flourished for me.

As I previously mentioned, my new friend Karen also lived at the residential treatment facility. Karen was a very friendly, outgoing, energetic, motivated person. This is how I saw myself too, except I didn't have the confidence she had, and I suppose I wasn't really outgoing. She had friends at the residential treatment facility who got together regularly, and she invited me into their group. I loved it. Honestly, they have no idea how much they meant to me. Once a week we would get together and put together scrapbooks. There were mainly five of us: Karen, me, Jessica, Christina, and Amelia. We did everything together. We all had the same job at the same place, so we had a lot in common already. This scenario created an opportunity for me to engage with them and have general discussions more naturally instead of me trying to find ways to fit in, like I had always had to do in my younger days. We planned trips together, we threw parties together, we took walks together. I became very close with them. In a way, they became my family. This was my life for five years, and I was on top of the world. This was the first time in my life I truly belonged in a friend group; I was one of them.

Then, like everything else, the situation changed. One by one, we left the residential treatment facility and went on to live and work in other arenas. I was devastated when this started happening; I've always struggled with big changes anyway, and my friends leaving made me feel like I was being left behind. Karen left first. I told her that I didn't like that she was moving, that things wouldn't be the same, that I'd never see her. She said they would be, that she would come to our regular weekly scrapbooking nights, and it would be just like she had never left. At first, she did, but then she'd skip a week here, two weeks there, until she stopped coming altogether. I felt a huge piece of me leave with her when she moved away.

As a group, we maintained our friendships, but the times we spent together became fewer and farther between. As I write this, I can say that it's been seven years since we've all been together, a fact that's actually very emotional for me. I'm literally sobbing as I write this because being in that community, having the close friendships with those women, I can't put it into words. I was one of them. That was the first time I belonged in that way. I attached myself to them because they showed me the love and affection I desperately wanted and needed while I was growing up and had never had in a friend-ship community. I thought I would have them all for life.

It's funny how our childhood traumas can have an impact on our lives for such a long time, how they can be quietly stored within us, how they can cause us to feel struggles years later that stem from seeds that were implanted so long ago. I attached to these women. I sought out their love and affection. I was enthralled by the feeling of belonging.

I feel like I could pick up the phone right now and call any one of them. In my heart, we are all still as close today as we were back then; we could pick up right where we left off with the same lev-el of acceptance and friendship still intact. That's how it would be on my end anyway. It's not necessarily the same on theirs. Karen wouldn't answer. Jessica wouldn't answer. Christina never answers when anyone calls her, but she would eventually call back. I'm not sure if Amelia would answer, but she would eventually probably call me back. Out of all of us, I have been able to maintain friendships without missing much of a beat with Christina and Amelia, no matter how much time goes by without talking to each other.

Let's talk about Karen, about the impact her friendship had on me. After all, she brought me to these wonderful women.

This friendship was a strong one, unbreakable even. After we moved away from the residential treatment facility, it wasn't uncommon for us to go long periods of time without speaking with each other but knowing that we were still there, still solid. Karen always seemed to understand the workings of things as a whole system, where I typically couldn't see past my piece of it. I always admired that about her.

One day I was thinking about Karen, and I realized I hadn't heard from her in a while. During that lapse, I had taken in four siblings so that they could stay together while their mom went into rehab, which is always heavy on my heart, by the way. I had reached out on Facebook and asked for help with some things I needed for the kids, and I didn't hear from Karen. I didn't think much of it until after the fact, but Karen worked with foster children as a career, so it made me start wondering why I hadn't heard from her when I was basically fostering those kids. So, I called her; she didn't answer. I sent her a text message and asked her if she was mad at me. *I always thought that people were mad at me, even when there was no logical reason to think that they would be; that I must've done something wrong. I suppose this is a result of my childhood struggles, always being held accountable for things that I had no idea about.* She responded and told me that she wasn't mad at me, that she just didn't want to be my friend anymore, that she wanted people around her who wanted to see her succeed, and that I wasn't one of those people. What? I literally had no idea what she was talking about; I was so confused. I felt like a train had run me over. I wanted to discuss it with her, but she wouldn't talk to me. That was it. She left me just like that. No warning, nothing. She was just gone from my life. This unbreakable friendship had broken.

This reopened old wounds, uncovered the past abandonments I felt I had healed from. It intensified the unresolved grief from my childhood that I believed I had overcome. The pain of that, it was unbelievable, unfathomable. It was like hearing every goodbye ever said to me all at the same time.

In typical fashion for me, I couldn't let it go. I went over it a million times in my head, trying to figure out how I caused this friendship to end. What could I have possibly done? How did I mess this up? How could a friendship that was so strong for so many years, 18 years to be exact, just end so abruptly, with not even a discussion, and in such a cold way? Then I thought of one situation that happened that was the only possible reason I could think of. I was working at my second program, Haven Home for Girls, which was struggling financially to stay open. Karen worked for another agency where she was pretty high up in management. I was talking on the phone with Christina when I saw an article on Facebook about how the agency Karen was working for was partnering with and financially assisting an agency that was similar to mine, and Karen was leading the cause. I was shocked to see this. Furthermore, this cause was right in our town. I was so taken aback. Why would she assist a different agency, and why would she not even tell me about it? Also, the selfish part of me was asking, "Why was she helping them in this manner and not me?" I was so upset about the whole situation. I guess Christina must have told Karen what I said about it. That is the only thing I can think of that happened. To be clear, I never said I didn't want her to succeed; I never even felt that way, ever. Honestly, I was mostly upset because she didn't tell me about it herself; I found out on Facebook.

The fact of the matter is, this wasn't the first time she had done something like this to me, and I was venting about it to Christina. Am I not allowed to have feelings about it? Why is it okay for her to have feelings and not me? I guess I just feel these things more deeply than everyone else.

As time passed and I thought about it more thoroughly, I developed a different perspective. I realized that throughout our friendship I was always focused on me, on how I was growing and how I was achieving. I was always chasing my next goal and making decisions to make sure I could achieve them. I was so focused on everything that was going on with me that I never stopped to really think about what was going on with her. Of course, I didn't realize this at the time. I mean, this way of thinking was ingrained in me; there's no plan B, remember? Now, don't get me wrong, we shared a lot with each other, and I was always compassionate and caring with her, with everyone for that matter, but my main focus was always on me, as I was programmed that way because I had always had to rely on myself. Additionally, anything negative toward me that happened with my friends, ever, since childhood, I took personally. I made this situation, the situation of her helping the other agency, about me instead of realizing that it was another success for her. I should have been showing her praise and offering her encouragement. This wasn't intentional; I didn't even realize this about myself until I started writing this book. The thing is, I always expected Karen to succeed, which she has. She said to me in a message one time after she decided to not be my friend anymore that I wasn't happy to see her succeed. I can't remember if she said I wanted to see her fail, but that was the message I got from that. I've spent a lot of time thinking about that and trying to understand why she would ever think such a thing about me. I can't even express what a gut punch that was to me, the tears I've shed over the loss of this friendship, the disbelief I have felt and had to work through because of this loss. She was my constant. I could call her with anything that I was going through, and she was there for me, until she wasn't. I think this happened because I made it all about me. I miss her so much. The reality is, though, that she left me in the same fashion I am accustomed to, abruptly.

Amelia and I became pretty close friends when we lived at the residential treatment facility. We lived across the road from each other. We spoke every day, several times a day. We knew everything about each other. We've maintained a friendship, but we don't see each other very often anymore. I feel like I'm the one who always reaches out, so it makes me think that I care about it more than she does. Who knows, maybe she just has a lot going on and it's not about me at all. I wouldn't know, though, because I haven't spoken with her. Maybe I take this too personally too.

Jessica and I were never super close, but I always enjoyed spending time with her. When I took the foster kids in, she gathered a ton of stuff for them. It was so nice of her, and I appreciated it so much. I've messaged her a few times, though, and have not ever gotten a return response. She and Karen were always really close, so maybe she just took sides in this, and that is why I haven't heard back from her.

Christina and I remain pretty good friends. We've worked together and vacationed together since we left the residential treatment facility. She is a lot of fun, and I love being around her. I actually was able to meet up with her last year and catch up. It was so great to see her. I don't hear from her much either, though, but I know she's just a phone call, or call back, away.

I find it strange that I don't hear from any of them anymore. They say that people grow apart as time goes by, but I don't know. Amelia was going to plan a get-together with all of us at her house a couple of years ago; we even talked about maybe going to her vacation home. I think she felt like she was in the middle of things in planning this, though, because Karen and I aren't friends anymore. I can understand that, I guess. I never heard anything more about getting together, though, so I'm honestly thinking that maybe they all got together without me.

I saw this Christmas ornament the other day that one could buy that has a group of friends sitting together; it can be individualized with the name of each friend under each person; it reads something like "Best friends 'til the end." I instantly thought of my group of friends from the residential treatment facility and thought what a great gift this would be to get for each of us to hang on our trees. The smile and happiness I felt in that moment brought such joy as I thought of each of them, of the laughs we shared, of our times together, but it only lasted for about ten seconds. Then the reality of the situation reared the ugly truth of it. Karen doesn't want to be my friend anymore. I haven't heard from Jessica since January of 2023. As I write this, it's been 36 months since I heard from her. I've messaged her a couple of times since, but she never responded. Amelia and I were planning to get together; that was last April, 21 months ago. She was going to look at her schedule so we could choose a date; she never got back to me. I've messaged her a couple of times since, wishing her a happy Mother's Day and another time letting her know I was thinking about her, but I haven't heard back from her either. Christina and I do talk every now and then, but not very often. I want to think they're just busy, too busy to maintain contact. But then I think, I'm busy too. I have a full-time job, a ten-year-old daughter, I'm busy with my church, and I run a nonprofit organization. I'm busy too, yet I make time for them. Why don't they make time for me? So, I guess deep down I don't believe they are too busy, and the deep-rooted childhood brokenness creeps in and makes me think that I've managed to push them away the same way I pushed friends away when I was a child; that at my core I am incapable of maintaining their friendships. I mean, I realize that we don't all live next door to each other anymore like we used to, but that shouldn't matter. I put myself out there time and time again, and for what?

These friendships that were so special and important to me are no longer what they used to be. This fact resonates within me and attaches itself to the inadequacies that I have felt at my core since childhood. It exemplifies my perceived inability to matter to other people. These people who I thought were my closest friends, who I counted on, they've left me too.

So, then I think that the Christmas ornament is not a good buy for us.

CHAPTER THIRTY-FOUR

A HOME IN EACH OTHER

Three people come to mind when I think about my best long-term friends: Savannah, Olivia, and Angelica.

Savannah

I've already spoken about Savannah. She was my saving grace in high school and throughout adulthood, though as we got older, we took different paths. As a result, we didn't see each other much at all. We never lost the close bond, though, that we shared with each other.

Savannah got really sick, and I'm heartbroken to say that she died. It'll be three years in August. She left me, but not by choice. If I had one more day to spend with her, I would tell her how she saved me, how she changed my life, how her acceptance and friendship were a light that will never dim. She is forever in my heart. May she rest in peace.

Olivia

After I moved in with Patrick Sr., I started working in the deli at a local grocery store. That's when I met Olivia. She was outgoing, engaging, and witty. While she was training me, she told me not to "steal all of her boyfriends." She was so funny; she always made me laugh. I felt comfortable around her and in my new position with her by my side.

As we got to know each other, I found that she knew the same people I did from the neighborhood and that she lived only about five minutes away from me. I also learned that she had suffered significant losses in her life, just as I had. I was content around her; she was easy to open up to. We bonded rather quickly.

Olivia and I understand each other in a way that feels indestructible. We know each other's thoughts and feelings without having to speak. She is truly my platonic soulmate, my person. I knew this from the moment I shared my brokenness with her, and she got it. She understood exactly what I was feeling. I can be my true self with her, down to my deepest, rawest emotions, the parts of me I wouldn't want anyone to see; she already knows them.

We hurt the same, love the same, think the same, process the same, conquer the same. When times are great, I know I can count on her to celebrate with me. When times are hard, I know I can count on her to talk, support, or just listen. She knows that I am always here to do the same for her.

These qualities are similar to what I suspect it is like to have a mother. Someone who is always there for me, who doesn't judge me, who supports me, who loves me through my darkest times, who celebrates my victories with me. I am fortunate to have found these qualities in this friendship.

When I left Patrick, she was there, loading up my car. When I miscarried, she sat at the hospital with me for hours and brushed my hair. I don't know why, but that simple act was so calming, so comforting. When I opened my first group home, she was right there, working alongside me to help it succeed. When I was suffering through postpartum depression, she showed up and cleaned my house. She has been through the best and worst times of my life with me. At times, we would randomly decide to take last-minute trips, to Virginia Beach, Niagara Falls, Cedar Point, anywhere, and we'd just pack up the car and go. No matter how last minute or how crazy the idea, we explored them together. I could go on and on. She was heaven-sent.

We have been friends for over 30 years now. She is my ride-or-die friend.

Angelica

Friendly. Caring. Compassionate. Loyal. Honest. Consistent. Happy. Understanding. These are just some of the words I could use to describe the friend I have found in Angelica. She has been by my side through thick and thin, always supportive, and has never given up on me. She is my rock.

It was college orientation. As I've mentioned, I hadn't had the best experience in high school when it came to making friends or feeling accepted. *Here we go again* was the thought I had running through my mind as I entered the student union. I looked around at the hundreds of people who were already seated. I was awkward, nervous, and self-conscious, as usual. I scanned the room for a seat. A girl sitting at the end of one of the tables spoke up and invited me to sit with her. That is when I met Angelica.

Her kindness instantly relieved my worries. We started talking a little bit, trying to get to know each other. She made me feel like maybe I wasn't going to have to navigate the day alone.

We formed a friendship quickly. Of course, I always made friends quickly, but this was different. We were both studying elementary education, and as it turned out, she only lived about 15 minutes away from me, which is worth noting since the college was 45 minutes away from our homes. We started doing everything together. We scheduled our classes together, carpooled, skipped classes together to grab breakfast, studied together, you name it. Occasionally, we even joined clubs together. One time, we joined the college's acting company and starred in Snow White. I was Snow White; can you believe it!? I was chosen for the lead role.

We became inseparable, sharing our lives through boyfriends, breakups, marriages, the births of our children, you name it. Side by side. Of course, we had our fair share of fights and disagreements, but they never stopped us from being there for each other. Even when we were upset, we always had each other's backs.

When I miscarried, she skipped her classes and sat with me at the hospital. She didn't need to say anything; her presence was enough.

When I got married for the first time, she was in my wedding. When I got married for the second time, she was in that wedding too. I didn't ask her to be in any more of my weddings. Frankly, I was embarrassed to be getting married over and over again. But she never judged me for it.

I moved about 40 minutes away from Angelica when my two oldest kids were little. It slowed our friendship down a little bit. We didn't see each other as often as we would've liked, but we still spoke regularly and maintained a close connection.

There were times when I wasn't a good friend to her, when I was downright mean. During those times, I felt justified. But looking back, those situations just seem silly. Why would I ever treat anyone that way? Why would she still want to be around me after I was so unkind? I am forever grateful that she has a forgiving heart because she never gave up on me. Our friendship was strong enough to withstand those trials. Once we would talk through things, we would put it behind us and pick up right where we left off, as if nothing had even happened. I suppose that's what an unconditional friendship looks like.

We've always found ourselves in the most ridiculous situations. In college, we were raising money for the acting company, so we made and sold pepperoni rolls. We got into an argument about them, but we both still showed up at school the next day to sell them together.

Another time, we sold candy bars. Since it was Halloween, we decided it would be a great idea to sell them to people waiting in lines for haunted houses. It was all fun and games until we found ourselves in a rough neighborhood with people aggressively approaching our car. That was scary.

Then there was the apple cider sale. We wanted to sell cider but didn't have enough apples, so we drove around knocking on random doors, asking people if we could pick their apples. When we finally filled up the truck bed, we took them to a cider press, made cider, and then stood on the side of the road to sell it.

Most recently, we volunteered at the baseball stadium to raise money for our church and my nonprofit. We attended a training session, but midway through, we realized it wasn't meant for volunteers, it was for employees. So, we tried to sneak out. One door led to another, and before we knew it, we were locked outside of the stadium, but inside the locked gates, unable to get back inside. It was dark, and we couldn't find a way out or back inside. We took selfies, laughed until we almost cried, and then panicked when nobody from the training would answer their phones. Eventually, we flagged down a random guy on the street and asked him to find someone to rescue us. When the worker finally let us back in, she didn't even ask what happened; never even questioned why we were where we were. She just led us right back to the training. So much for our great escape.

I could go on forever with stories like these. We've had a lot of fun and creative problem-solving moments together.

Now I live just five minutes away from Angelica again. Moving near her is one of the best decisions I've ever made. We see each other all the time, belong to the same church, and continue to share most of our lives. Her family is my family, and I love being a part of it.

Angelica is everything anyone could hope for in a friend. I am beyond blessed to have her in my life, as my rock. This is one friend who has not left, and hopefully never will.

CHAPTER THIRTY-FIVE

MARRIAGE

Marriage. A lifelong, covenantal relationship between a man and a woman, established by God. A voluntary union characterized by faithfulness, sacrificial love, and joy.

Growing up, I had my own perceptions of marriage. My mom and dad's marriage didn't model what I should be striving for; I knew that for sure. My aunt wasn't married and lived as a single mother, so that didn't give me what I needed either. I gained a little bit of insight when I saw couples at church wearing matching outfits every Sunday and by seeing the "perfect" families with a husband, a wife, and their happy children. That looked nice, but how did they get to that point? I was lost. I knew I wanted a loving, lifelong marriage, but I had no idea how to have that or how to appreciate the beginnings of that type of love. The most influential thing I had to go by were the movies where men went to great lengths to win the love of the women they adored. I wanted that. I wanted someone to feel that way about me, to put me first, to make me feel like I was the most important person in their entire world, to make me feel worthy of being a wife. In my mind, that was the goal. And if I was lucky enough to find someone who wanted to marry me, I was determined to do everything in my power to make that marriage last a lifetime. I didn't want my children to grow up in a broken home like I did. I was never going to break up my family.

In this, I failed.

They say that those raised on love see life differently than those raised on survival. I think that applies here. Instead of dating, I just married. Then I'd battle internal conflicts between fighting to make my marriage work and making sure I left the situation before they could leave me. I am currently on my fifth marriage, fourth legally; one of the marriages was never finalized because the paperwork wasn't turned in to the courthouse. I have my reasons for ending each one, and some of them are legitimate, but that doesn't make it acceptable or even okay. Instead, it's embarrassing, humiliating, even gut-wrenching to think of the disservice I did to my children, to those men, and to myself. When I think about each of them, the men I built connections with, made promises to, gave my all to, then ultimately left, I feel ashamed.

Sometimes, I picture us together and think of the good qualities they had, and I smile. Then I wonder how different my life would be if I had fought harder to fix what was broken instead of shutting them out one by one. There are many things I could have done differently in each marriage. But instead, I ended them. I cut each man out of my life before they had a chance to leave me. I was not going to allow myself to be vulnerable enough to be abandoned again.

So yes, I failed them. But worse, I failed my children. And that's the hardest part. I beat myself up about it constantly because I never wanted that for them. I pray that they don't follow in my footsteps in this regard, that when they marry, it's forever. That they are 100% committed and that they fight for their marriages instead of giving up on them like I did.

CHAPTER THIRTY-SIX

SAVING THE WORLD

Although I have been through a lot of traumatic events, I have fought hard not to let any of them define me, although, unconsciously, I suppose they have. Purposefully, however, I've focused on helping others. And although I never realized it until recently, I've also focused on proving my worth to the world, proving that I matter, that I am valuable.

Coming from a childhood without my mother by my side; a childhood that lacked affection, emotional connection, and support, I knew I had to set goals for myself and do whatever it took to accomplish them. I had no safety net, no one to fall back on. As I said before, I was my own Plan A and Plan B. From a young age, I understood that. It made me struggle to trust that others would show up for me; I had to survive on my own.

Imagine growing up feeling that way. To call it terrible is an understatement. But living in that tumultuous environment shaped me. It gave me the ability to see others through compassionate eyes, to feel their pain because I had been through my own. It also made me question everything, recognize loopholes, and see the good in people no matter how much bad they showed me.

I had, and still have, so much energy, love, and care to give, and when faced with the choice to sink or swim, I have always chosen, and continue to choose, to swim.

The trauma of being separated from my siblings has always weighed heavily on my heart. I have long dreamed of creating a space where siblings facing separation could stay together. I've even taken in siblings so that they could stay together. Maybe that dream is my way of rewriting my own past. I considered being a foster parent and taking in sibling groups, but my own life circumstances never quite allowed for it. With five children of my own, it wasn't an option for a long time. Now, I live in a small ranch-style farmhouse with just three bedrooms, one for my husband and me, one for my daughter, and one extra.

So instead, I formed a nonprofit organization, Harbor Momentum, with the focus on keeping families together. Through Harbor Momentum, we formed the Laura Walker Foundation, named after my mother. Through this foundation, we focus on keeping siblings together. We offer financial awards to selected individuals who have taken in foster sibling groups. Our future plans include creating those spaces I've longed for, where siblings can safely stay together as opposed to being separated. I don't have all the logistics figured out yet, but I know in time I will, and it will all come together.

When Vincent and I became house parents at the residential treatment facility, we lived with our own children in an apartment connected to the boys' home. For five years, this was our life. We were their "stand-in" parents, guiding them, teaching them rules, playing games, taking them to events, cooking for and with them, and helping them become productive members of society. That was my first real chance to give back, to help other people who were broken like I was. Sure, their wounds were different than mine, but beneath it all, we felt the same things.

I loved that job. It wasn't perfect, but what job is? It opened my eyes to even more ways I could help. That's when I decided I wanted to do more.

I formed my first nonprofit organization, Moms Without Moms. At first, it offered a support group for women like me, women navigating life without their mothers. Haylee played a big part in this with me. We held monthly meetings, shared stories, and supported one another. Through my work, I saw another need: at-risk teenage mothers. These girls consisted of a combination of both delinquent and dependent teenagers who needed to live away from their homes by court order. Young girls who were being separated from their babies because no one had a place to keep them together. Many of these girls would be in placement, go to the hospital to have their baby, and a day or two later would be returned to their placement, **without their baby**. Let that sink in. **Without their baby.**

That broke my heart.

So, I expanded Moms Without Moms and opened a group home for pregnant and parenting teenagers.

The home was beautiful. It was an old doctor's office in Grove City, Pennsylvania. Each exam room became a bedroom. I secured contracts with 17 counties across the state. We could house a total of up to 16 people, any combination of young women and babies, at a time. These girls had nowhere else to go, and we were there to guide them. Among other things, we taught parenting classes, helped them find jobs, and supported them throughout school. But most importantly, we gave them a safe place where they could stay with their babies. We created a space that allowed them to stay together.

I named the program The Laura Walker Project, after my mother.

Most of the girls were grateful for the opportunity, knowing the alternative was separation. Some struggled with the rules, with the reality that they couldn't just leave whenever they wanted since they were court-ordered. We did the best we could to help them see the bigger picture.

After five years, The Laura Walker Project closed. I had started the program on faith, with no money of my own. A generous local businessman, a true pro-life advocate, bought the building and renovated it for us. He supported us through countless struggles, but when he decided to part ways, we weren't in a financial position to buy the building from him. I was devastated. But I didn't give up.

I partnered with a friend and opened another home, Haven Home for Girls, near Harrisburg. It operated for six years until financial issues and other struggles forced its closure. To be honest, I wonder sometimes if God stepped in and made that decision for me because I had been struggling to balance the program with my own family's needs. I lived four and a half hours away from that home. I had adopted my youngest daughter just three years earlier and had two teenagers at home. I tried to be present for them while running Haven Home for Girls, but I was stretched quite thin. Maybe closing it was God's way of forcing me to realign my priorities.

Still, I struggled with feeling like a failure. I often still do. I've replayed every decision from both homes over and over again, wondering what I could have done differently, imagining the additional girls I could have kept together with their babies had the homes stayed open. And then I think about all the young lives I was able to help through those homes. We, the staff and I, made a tremendous impact for each mom and baby. That's not failure; that's victory.

It's been fifteen years since The Laura Walker Project closed and eight and a half years since Haven Home for Girls closed. Not a week goes by that I don't think about working with those girls from both programs. I've considered opening another program, but I hesitate. I wonder, would people really take me seriously after two closures? Or am I just afraid of feeling like a failure again?

Maybe I'm not done yet.

Harbor Momentum is growing. We've begun to support foster families who have taken in sibling groups, in an effort to increase awareness of this need and to encourage others to open their hearts and homes. Additionally, we've launched a sponsorship program that allows individuals to support local families in need, like the overseas sponsorship programs, but right here at home, and sponsoring families instead of one child in a family. We originally started this program with the focus on sponsoring individual children, and have sponsored 97 children! We recently changed our focus from "child" to "family," as we realized that supporting the family as a whole allows for a better family unit to succeed, and it better aligns with our mission of keeping families together. A major goal we are working towards is to purchase homes where we can provide spaces to keep sibling groups together when they need to live away from their homes.

Who knows what future years will bring. I know we're just getting started, and I can't wait to see how this organization continues to flourish.

CHAPTER THIRTY-SEVEN

LET THEM

"Let them."

This phrase has recently taken on a life of its own, almost as if it has become a movement. Two simple words. People are getting them tattooed on their bodies, using them as a mantra to move on, to let people treat them however they choose, and to simply not care. It sounds like a great idea. I would love to be able to do that. But how do people actually accomplish that? How do you go about your daily life and not feel the pain and hurt that others cause you? How do you stand in front of those people and not feel emotions?

Perhaps I care too much, engage more than I should, feel things too deeply. I can't imagine ever getting to a point where I could just 'let them'.

I've spoken before about cutting people out of my life. I've done that, and I've done it easily and without looking back. Doing so made me feel relieved, but it also made me feel a bit sad, and even guilty. I did it because I had to do it in order to clear my head enough to move forward mentally, emotionally, and physically.

For example, when I cut Aunt Judith and that life out, I did it because I had to. I couldn't carry all of that with me while I was trying to make something of myself and find emotional stability. It was a necessity. However, that separation didn't mean I forgot about that life or those people. I still cared about them. I didn't want anything bad to happen to them. I wished them well, but from a distance.

I feel the concept of 'let them' is similar to cutting people out of your life, but different. To me, letting them means continuing on with life, perhaps even engaging with those individuals, but ignoring how they treat you, and feeling nothing. I can't see myself ever being able, or even wanting to be able, to do that. I suppose some might call it professionalism in the workplace, but I wouldn't want that in my personal life.

This past Thanksgiving, I cooked a huge Thanksgiving meal, four turkeys stuffed with homemade stuffing, sixty pounds of mashed potatoes, and gravy. I invited all of my family, a lot of my friends, and my whole church. I called it Friendsgiving.

This was the third annual Friendsgiving I've hosted. Our church has a beautiful hall for events like this, so that's where I held it. I sent out save the dates in February so everyone could mark their calendars. The event was scheduled for November 2nd, earlier in the month this year to avoid interfering with people's Thanksgiving plans, since last year some couldn't attend because it was too close to the holiday.

I spent the entire day cooking, setting up the hall, making drinks, preparing stuffing, stuffing the turkey, peeling and cooking mashed potatoes, doing everything imaginable to prepare for everyone's arrival. The aroma of roasting turkey filled the air. My body ached from standing all day, but the excitement kept me going.

My rock, Angelica, was there. Two friends from church, Martha and Abigail, helped, along with my niece and her boyfriend. My son, Patrick, came for a little while to lend a hand. My husband had to work but helped at the end. I couldn't have done it without every single one of them. I cannot express enough how much I appreciate what they did. It took the entire day, and it was exhausting, but it was worth every minute.

Some people who came brought delicious desserts and side dishes to share. Everything was amazing. I enjoyed seeing every single person who attended. Even a high school classmate I hadn't seen since graduation showed up. It was a wonderful group of people, and we were blessed to share that time and meal together.

For this, I am thankful. Truly thankful.

I do not want to take anything away from the joy I felt and the togetherness we shared.

But here's the flip side.

Where was everyone else?

A great number of family members didn't even bother to respond to the invitation. They didn't come. Only a few of my other friends came. Of my church family, only fourteen people attended. A few others from church stopped by during the day for various reasons but said they wouldn't be staying for dinner, and didn't.

So where were they?

Where was everyone?

Why didn't they want to come and share a meal with each other, with me?

Looking around that room, it felt much larger than in previous years. The emptiness of the seats stood out. The room felt quieter than it should have. And once I realized that so many of the people I cherished weren't there, an uneasiness settled in my stomach.

My feelings were hurt on a level that's difficult to describe.

And so, here I am, in my fifties, still feeling, when triggered, that insecurity that is deep-rooted within me: unimportant, unwanted, unworthy of people's time.

It makes me feel as though all the positive changes I've made, all the recreating of myself, all the nurturing of friendships, were for nothing. As if I had been experiencing these relationships through a lens of what I imagined them to be rather than what they actually were. One-sided.

I tried to process the hurt. I talked with Angelica. I made excuses for everyone. I prayed.

But nothing helped in that moment.

When faced with rejection like that, my first instinct is always to isolate. To sit alone on my couch, let the pain wash over me, and cry. Then, I refocus. I remind myself of the blessings in my life, of the true friendships I have, and I regroup. I stand tall again.

So, tell me, how do you just let them?

I don't get it.

I don't think I ever will.

My first inclination was to cut them all out. To never speak to them again. To stop attending the church I've been part of for so many years. To never text or call my friends again. To delete my Facebook.

But then I think, I can't do that; that's not who I am.

Maybe I want to leave that door open just in case someone ever finds it important enough to walk through.

Or maybe I leave the door open so when someone is in need, they'll remember that I am here for them, because no matter what, I am here for them.

I know that sounds ridiculous. I know it is ridiculous.

But I also know, deep down, that this is why I don't shut it all down.

Because, even though at times they don't seem to care much for me, I still care for them.

Perhaps, if I could just 'let them', I'd finally be free from the hold they have on me.

CHAPTER THIRTY-EIGHT

REFLECTIONS

Intimacy

It's funny how experiences change you. *Choosing* to be intimate with someone for the first time is a new level of independence for someone who has had that decision taken from them. I remember thinking that when I realized that I had a choice, that I could say yes or no. It was up to me! I remember the anticipation, the desire to feel that closeness with the man I was in love with, to express that true act of love. That is supposed to be the deepest and most intimate connection you can form with a person, something reserved for the one you fall deeply in love with, the one you wish to spend the rest of your life with.

But it turns out that it's not always like that for people who have been exploited.

For me, intimacy is in the kiss. Kissing someone is magical. It's not simply about lips touching, it's the *desire* to kiss, the butterflies that flutter in my stomach when it finally happens. That's where the deep, intimate bond happens for me. I assume this is because I was never made to kiss anyone during the times of exploitation.

The Absent Mother

My feelings about my mother's murder have evolved over the years. I've always hated the fact that she was taken from me, of course, and that I had to grow up without her. That I still face situations where I long for the presence, connection, and support of her that I've imagined would be present, that I never had the unconditional love that a mother gives. I've fantasized about what it would have been like to have her. Since I can't remember her, I created different versions of her in my mind, versions of who she might have been if she had lived.

I imagine a supportive mom who would have loved her grandchildren, who would have guided me through my struggles. A fun mom who would have pushed me on the swings and danced in the rain. A caring mom who would have comforted me whenever I needed it. A classy mom who wore heels and business clothes to work as a bank teller. An adventurous mom who would have taken me to see the world.

In every version, she is happy, fun, and perfect.

I wonder where I would have lived growing up, what friendships I would have had, who I would have married. The versions of her I've created are everything I could dream of: beautiful, encouraging, patient, funny, and always there for me. I picture us shopping together, cooking together, and being the best of friends. I could go on and on.

Not being able to remember her is possibly the saddest part of all. It's what makes it so difficult to find peace with the situation.

The fact remains: I didn't get the chance to have my mother, and that is ultimately my father's fault.

I'm angry at him. The kind of anger that words cannot fully capture.

Even now, I feel it.

He took my mother from me.

And yet, When I see his handwriting, I feel sorrow and understanding for him. When I think about the loss *he* felt, the grief he carried, over losing his children *again*, I can empathize with him.

One thing my life's traumas have taught me is that I see *eight* sides of every situation, no matter what it is. Things are not simply black and white. Reading his letters only reinforced that for me.

I chose a long time ago to forgive him. That doesn't mean I agree with what he did or am excusing his cowardly act. I *definitely* am not. It simply means that I had to let go of the burden of unforgiveness.

Misunderstood

I've learned the hard way that the way I see things is often vastly different from how others view them. I've come to accept that my mind naturally operates differently.

For one, I can watch a traumatic situation play out right in front of me without being shocked or surprised by it, which allows me to react to it in a way that others cannot because I don't get caught up in the emotions of it. On the flip side of that though, I will feel for the victim so deeply that I carry the weight of the pain I imagine they are dealing with with me for long periods of time. Some situations I have never been able to let go of, like Shasta Groene and Elizabeth Smart. I don't even know them, but I still carry their pain and suffering with me. The situations involving children always affect me the most.

Two, my processing speed is usually about five steps ahead of most people around me. While this might sound like an advantage, it has created countless misunderstandings, both in my personal relationships and professional interactions. I rarely take things at face value. Instead, I dissect conversations, carefully analyzing each word, each gesture, and every subtle shift in body language. While someone speaks, my mind races ahead, piecing together their perspective, motivations, and potential reactions. When I finally respond, it can be as though I'm addressing a conclusion that the other person hasn't even considered yet. This leaves them confused or defensive, wondering how I arrived at that point, when they're still processing the words spoken only moments ago.

I know now that my way of thinking didn't appear by chance. It's a direct result of growing up in an environment where my every action and decision was rigorously questioned, picked apart, and scrutinized. It's also the inevitable outcome of enduring repeated loss, abandonment, and heartbreak. These experiences have taught me to discern the true intentions of others, to anticipate disasters, to prepare for worst-case scenarios, and to guard myself fiercely against disappointment.

Yet there's an unexpected strength in this. Few things startle or scare me. Life can throw curveballs, and I simply adapt, taking things as they come and figuring out solutions, one quick yet carefully crafted step at a time. I've learned resilience not because life was gentle, but precisely because it was not.

The past undeniably shaped me, molded my perceptions, and altered the course of my life, but crucially, it does not own me. For a long time, I believed healing meant rewriting my story, erasing the parts that hurt the most, and crafting a better, happier narrative. But now, I see clearly that true healing isn't about rewriting the past; it's about making peace with the story exactly as it unfolded. It's acknowledging the raw truth, accepting the pain, and understanding that some wounds never fully heal. And perhaps that isn't even the point. Perhaps the real purpose is to learn how to carry these wounds with grace, to bear them without allowing them to define or weigh me down.

So, from here, I choose to move forward, not as the person shaped solely by pain and loss, but as someone defined by resilience, clarity, and strength. I move forward, not bound to who I was, but empowered by who I consciously choose to become.

CHAPTER THIRTY-NINE

THE STAGES OF GRIEF IN MY OWN WORDS

I first learned about the five stages of grief in college. As I studied them, I tried to trace my own progression through each stage, wondering if this model accurately reflected how I had processed the loss of my mother and my father.

The Five Stages of Grief

According to the Kübler-Ross model, those experiencing grief after a sudden loss go through five emotional stages:

1. **Denial** - Initially, individuals believe the loss is a mistake and cling to a false reality. Some may isolate themselves to avoid confronting the truth.

   For me, denial lasted a long time, at least a couple of years. I remember, as I previously mentioned, sitting in my third-grade classroom, staring at the door, waiting for my mother to come and pick me up, to tell me it was all a mistake. Any explanation that would have made her death untrue, I would have accepted.

2. **Anger** - When denial fades, frustration takes its place. This often leads to lashing out, blaming others, or questioning fairness.

I remember being very angry while living with Aunt Judith. "Why me?" and "It's not fair!" became my mantras. Nothing about the situation made sense, and the fact that no one would talk to me about it made it even worse. Why was I put on this earth just to endure such a traumatic life? What was the purpose of all this pain? Sometimes, I wonder if I've ever fully moved past this stage.

3. **Bargaining** - This stage involves attempts to negotiate or find a compromise, often with a higher power. People in grief may make promises to change if it means reversing or altering the reality of their loss.

   I don't recall ever being in this stage. I never tried to make a deal or offer up something in exchange for a different reality.

4. **Depression** - A deep sadness settles in as the weight of the loss becomes fully realized. People in this stage often feel despair, loneliness, and hopelessness.

   Depression has been a constant presence in my life. I wouldn't say I've ever fully moved past this stage either. I've never been suicidal, but I have struggled with long periods of darkness, where pulling myself out felt almost impossible. Some days were easier than others, but the heaviness never fully left me.

5. **Acceptance** - The final stage is about coming to terms with loss. It doesn't mean happiness or even full healing, but rather an understanding that life must go on.

   I have accepted that my mother and father are gone. The sadness hasn't disappeared, but I have come to terms with the reality of it. I don't have a choice.

Grief as Healing; A different way to look at the stages of grief

I've seen these stages reframed as the *stages of healing*. That shift in perspective makes sense to me. Healing from trauma isn't just about surviving grief, it's about learning to live with it.

1. **Denial to Awareness**
   Coming to terms with my mother's death was not an overnight

process. It took time, years even. Every person experience grief differently, but for me, reaching the point where I could say, "She's never coming back" was a small step toward healing.

2. **Anger to Reflection**
I still ask, "Why did this happen to me?" and "How is this fair? But I recognize that those questions don't lead anywhere. Instead, I try to ask, "How has this shaped me?" and "What have I learned from this?" Those are questions I can actually reflect upon and even answer.

3. **Bargaining to Letting Go**
While I never experienced bargaining in the traditional sense, I did live in a world of "what ifs." What if my mother hadn't gone to my father's house that day? What if they had never separated? What if we had never moved back to Pennsylvania? I spent years creating alternate realities in my head. But I no longer do that. I've let those thoughts go.

4. **Depression to Seeking Help**
Depression has been the hardest stage for me. It's been a companion for as long as I can remember. My first experience with counseling was in college. I poured out everything I had held inside for years, and for the first time, I felt lighter. I scheduled another session, but they assigned me to a different counselor, one who seemed distracted and uninterested. I never went back. Over the years, I have tried therapy again with different counselors, but none ever stuck. It always felt like a chore, so I stopped going. At one point, my doctor prescribed me antidepressants, but I didn't like how they made me feel, so I stopped taking those too. I wanted to learn how to deal with my emotions, not numb them.

Maybe my reluctance to seek help is part of why I still struggle with depression. Or maybe it's because I've always had to be strong, not just for myself but for everyone around me. The idea of being completely transparent with a counselor, of letting them see the dark corners of my mind, it terrifies me. Maybe that's why I haven't truly healed from this stage.

5. **Acceptance to Moving Forward**
   I have accepted that my parents are gone. That they are never coming back. It's a sadness that will never fully leave me. But I have also accepted that I can still live a meaningful life despite it.

I will never be the person I might have been if things had gone differently, but I am who I am because of everything I've survived. I'm strong, I'm independent, I care for and love others with all of my heart, I am a good mom, and my children are loved with every piece of me. Most importantly, perhaps, is that they know they are loved and accepted, and that I have their backs, no matter what. This proves that I have been able to overcome a significant amount of the trauma, and fallout from the trauma, that I endured as a child.

All of that has to count for something - for everything.

CHAPTER FORTY

THE STAGE OF ANGER

Let's talk about the anger stage. One thing I never hear people talk about is how angry you can become during the healing process. As a child growing up with Aunt Judith, I had no control over my life or anything in it. Any time Aunt Judith ridiculed me, belittled me, or made my feelings or needs seem insignificant, I would plunge deeper into a place of self-loathing, but I would also become angry.

One time, I broke my arm. Aunt Judith came to the school to pick me up and take me to the doctor. While we were sitting in the doctor's office, just the two of us, I worked up enough courage to ask her if she would take me to the cemetery to see my mom. I had been there a few times with her, but not very often. And nobody ever talked with me about my mom, so it was difficult to ask Aunt Judith to take me there. With anticipation, and the expectation that she would decline my request, I delicately asked the question. As expected, she instantly said no. No reason was given, no discussion was had, and no regard was shown for the feelings that led me to make this request. It was just *no*. I was so mad at her. I was overcome with indignation, resentment, and hostility. My heart raced, my muscles tensed, my eyes squinted, and my face felt heated due to the offense I was feeling. This was the response I had each time she treated me as insignificant.

I was faced with this situation quite often growing up. It hardened me. I remember feeling angry all the time; so angry that I wanted to beat people up, people who weren't even involved in any of my trauma. I just wanted to cause pain to another person. I'm not proud of having those feelings, but I'm bringing it up because I can't be alone in this. Thankfully, I never acted on them. I think I just wanted to be in control, and that was how I imagined I could achieve it. After all, those who hurt me were in control of me when my pain was inflicted.

In regards to being exploited, I never hear anyone talk about the unfathomable rage you can feel when you get old enough, or perhaps mature enough, to realize just how much you were taken advantage of, and for how long. I would be overcome with revulsion toward those who had caused me pain whenever I thought about it. I would feel like I was over it, healed from it, and then a scent, a vision, or even a familiar voice would come along, and all of those feelings would come rushing back. I would freeze in the moment, feeling a physical heaviness in my chest. Then I would gather myself, reminding myself that it was in the past; that I am safe now.

CHAPTER FORTY-ONE

MANIPULATION

Some experts say that girls and women who are sexually exploited tend to stay away from men. I can tell you that it can go either way. In my case, I sought out the attention of men, not in a promiscuous way, but in a way that ensured I could get attention from them when I wanted it. And I did.

Think about it: I had no support system at home. I had only one friend at school. I felt alone all the time and couldn't understand why nobody wanted me or wanted to be around me. The one man who was supposed to keep me safe had killed my mother. Then, the one who was nice to me had me performing sex acts on him. I didn't have a positive male role model to learn from, to show me how men were supposed to treat women.

I had learned how to gain attention from men, and I used those skills to get their attention where I could. Add to that the manipulation skills I had learned from Aunt Judith, and I was golden. I knew how to manipulate any situation in my favor. I felt empowered by this ability, like I could take control of my life and others. But I also felt conflicted because I wanted people to be around me because they *wanted* to be, not because I had manipulated them into it, so I made it a conscious point to not use these skills, even though I wanted to, and I knew I could.

I contemplated leaving this part out of the book but decided to include it because it affected the way I interact with men overall. And again, I cannot be alone in this.

CHAPTER FORTY-TWO

VINDICATION

I never thought about or expected anyone to apologize to me for the pain they had inflicted. I mean, Dad was dead, so he couldn't apologize. Beyond that, I was certain that I just had to deal with what I had gone through and get over it. So how do you handle that? How do you handle feeling so angry toward them?

I decided I didn't want to continue feeling that way; I didn't want to be angry all the time. So, I forgave Aunt Judith for everything; the way she treated me, the lies, the ridicule, the isolation. I forgave that young man for coercing me into performing sex acts on him. And I forgave my father for taking my mother from me and for ultimately ruining my childhood, my life. I chose to forgive them even though I had never received an apology. This was something I did for my own healing; I needed to let the weight of that go, and I can tell you it was worth it.

To my shock and surprise, as an adult, Aunt Judith did apologize to me, in her own way. We were on a camping trip. I had gone to camp with my cousins, the ones I grew up with, and their families. I didn't know Aunt Judith would be there, or I probably wouldn't have gone. We were sitting by our camps at a picnic table when it happened. She didn't say the words "I'm sorry," but she basically said that she did the best she could. I felt a kind of release when I heard her say that. I know that couldn't have been easy for her, and I appreciated the effort.

Interestingly enough, that young man apologized to me too. He came the whole way, from several hours away, to my house just to apologize, in person. He said he hadn't realized the effect it would have on me, that he never meant to hurt me. He hadn't been thinking about me. Honestly, if you think about it, he was a teenager; he was probably only thinking about himself. I know it was difficult for him to discuss what he had done to me with me. I appreciated the apology. Honestly, I felt a little embarrassed to be talking about it, even though I was the victim. I also felt relief, like it had come full circle and it was finally over. I never thought he was a terrible human being. I thought maybe he, too, was troubled, of course, I had these thoughts as an adult, after I had chosen to forgive him, even without the apology.

AUTHOR'S NOTE: A CURIOUS INVESTIGATION

Writing this memoir was a deeply personal process, a way to navigate the immense loss that shaped my life. But as I wrote, I began to see my story as part of something much larger, a reflection of a hidden reality. I found myself asking, 'How common is this, really?'

I felt compelled to understand the broader context of domestic violence, to see where my experience fit within the larger picture. So, I turned to the statistics. What I discovered was both unsettling and illuminating.

The numbers revealed a stark truth: intimate partner violence is far more prevalent than I had imagined. Each statistic represented a life touched by pain, a family torn apart. It wasn't just data; it was a reflection of the experiences many people endure in silence, as was my experience.

The research helped me understand that my trauma, while deeply personal, was not isolated. It was a part of a larger pattern, a shared experience of those affected by domestic violence. This realization brought a sense of understanding, but also a profound sadness.

I realized that by sharing my story, I could contribute to a vital conversation, a way to break the silence that often surrounds these issues. I could give someone the strength to remove themselves from a situation before it is too late for them. The statistics weren't just numbers on a page; they were a call to action.

Raising awareness is crucial. Domestic violence thrives in secrecy. By bringing these issues into the light, we can empower survivors and work towards change.

Sharing my story became a way to amplify the voices of those who have been silenced.

My memoir is a testament to resilience, a reminder that healing is possible even after great trauma. And it's a plea to recognize the devastating impact of domestic violence. By including these statistics, I hope to add weight to this important subject and inspire meaningful change in the lives of those most impacted by its destruction.

Here's what I found:

Intimate Partner Violence (IPV) is alarmingly prevalent:

As I delved into the research, one stark and undeniable truth emerged: Intimate Partner Violence (IPV) is alarmingly prevalent, a shadow that looms over far too many lives. It became clear that my father's act, while uniquely devastating to my own life, was not an isolated incident. The statistics painted a grim picture of a widespread crisis.

Research consistently shows that a significant portion of murders are committed by intimate partners. This isn't just a fleeting trend; it's a persistent, deeply rooted problem. According to numerous studies, women are disproportionately affected, bearing the brunt of this violence. The numbers reveal a disturbing pattern of control, abuse, and ultimately, lethal violence within the very spaces meant to be safe havens.

For example, data indicates that a shockingly large percentage of female homicide victims are killed by their current or former intimate partners. These aren't just faceless numbers; they represent mothers, sisters, daughters, and friends whose lives were violently cut short. It's a terrifying reality that the people who should be the most trusted and loving figures in a woman's life are often the ones who pose the greatest danger.

Furthermore, the research revealed the insidious nature of IPV, showing how it often escalates over time. It rarely begins with lethal violence; it starts with subtle forms of control, emotional abuse, and manipulation, gradually escalating to physical and sexual violence. This pattern makes it difficult for victims to recognize the danger they're in, as the abuse becomes normalized within their relationship.

I also learned that IPV is not limited to physical violence. It encompasses a wide range of abusive behaviors, including emotional, psychological, financial, and sexual abuse. This multifaceted nature of IPV makes it even more difficult to identify and address.

The data also highlighted the impact on children who witness or experience IPV. They are often left with deep emotional scars, witnessing violence that shatters their sense of safety and security. I understand this impact all too well.

Understanding the prevalence of IPV has been both eye-opening and deeply disturbing. It has given me a new perspective on my own experience, showing me that I am not alone in my pain, though I felt alone in it most of my life. I am hopeful that the sharing of my story will not only raise awareness but will encourage those who suffer from the devastating consequences of intimate partner violence to remove themselves from their situation.

The Impact on Children:

My research also turned a harsh light onto the devastating impact of domestic violence on children. The trauma experienced by children who witness or experience domestic violence, and especially those who lose a parent to homicide, is profound, leaving invisible scars that can last a lifetime. It's a reality I know intimately, having lived through the aftermath of such a devastating loss.

These children often become silent witnesses to a war waged within their own homes, a war they are powerless to stop. The constant tension, the fear, and the unpredictable outbursts of violence create an environment of chronic stress and anxiety. Children may witness physical assaults, hear verbal abuse, or feel the palpable tension that permeates the air when violence is imminent. This constant exposure to trauma disrupts their sense of safety and security, leaving them feeling vulnerable and helpless.

The loss of a parent to homicide adds another layer of complexity to their trauma. Not only do they grieve the loss of a loved one, but they also grapple with the violent nature of their death. The world becomes a terrifying and unpredictable place, where even those closest to them can inflict unimaginable harm.

These children often face long-term emotional, psychological, and social challenges. They may experience anxiety, depression, post-traumatic stress disorder (PTSD), and difficulty forming healthy relationships. They may struggle with academic performance, exhibit behavioral problems, or withdraw from social interactions. The trauma can affect their cognitive development, their ability to regulate their emotions, and their overall sense of well-being. I am a living testament to each of these conditions. One thing I did personally was literally pull my hair out in chunks on a regular basis.

The impact of witnessing or experiencing domestic violence can also lead to a cycle of violence, as children may learn that violence is an acceptable way to resolve conflict. They may become victims or perpetrators of violence in their own relationships.

My heart aches for these children, knowing the long and arduous journey they face. I understand the weight of the unspoken fears, the nightmares that haunt their sleep, and the constant feeling of being unsafe. It's a burden no child should ever have to bear.

The Hidden Nature of Domestic Violence:

One of the most disturbing aspects of my research was the realization of how deeply domestic violence remains hidden, shrouded in secrecy and shame. It's a silent epidemic, thriving in the shadows, where victims are often trapped in a cycle of abuse that no one else sees.

This veil of secrecy is often maintained by the abuser, who uses tactics of manipulation, control, and fear to silence their victims. They may isolate them from friends and family, monitor their communication, and threaten them with further violence if they speak out. The victim, often feeling trapped and helpless, may believe that no one will believe them or that they are somehow responsible for the abuse.

Shame also plays a significant role in keeping domestic violence hidden. Victims may feel ashamed of what is happening to them, believing that they are weak or that they have failed in some way. They may fear judgment from others, especially in communities where domestic violence is stigmatized.

This culture of silence makes it incredibly difficult to fully grasp the true extent of the problem. The statistics that are recorded, while alarming, likely represent only a fraction of the actual cases. Many incidents go unreported, either because victims are afraid to come forward or because they do not recognize the abuse as domestic violence.

The hidden nature of domestic violence also makes it difficult to provide adequate support and resources for victims. When abuse is hidden, it is harder for family, friends, and community members to intervene. This isolation can further exacerbate the victim's sense of helplessness and despair.

Understanding the hidden nature of domestic violence has been a sobering experience. It has reinforced my belief that we must break the silence and create a culture where victims feel safe to come forward. We must challenge the stigma and shame that surround domestic violence and provide support and resources for those who are suffering. Only then can we truly begin to address this pervasive and devastating problem.

The Numbers:

As I delved deeper into the research, I encountered a frustrating reality: obtaining accurate statistics on domestic violence on a global scale is incredibly challenging. This is due to a multitude of factors, including the varying ways different countries collect and report data, cultural stigma surrounding domestic violence, and the significant number of cases that go unreported.

The lack of standardized reporting methods across countries makes it difficult to compare data and get a clear picture of the global prevalence of domestic violence. Some countries may have robust systems for tracking these incidents, while others may have limited or no data collection at all. This inconsistency makes it challenging to assess the true magnitude of the problem on a worldwide scale.

Furthermore, cultural norms and stigma surrounding domestic violence can significantly impact reporting rates. In many societies, domestic violence is considered a private matter, and victims may be discouraged from reporting abuse due to fear of reprisal, shame, or social ostracism. This cultural silence can lead to a significant underestimation of the true extent of the problem.

The hidden nature of domestic violence also contributes to the difficulty in obtaining accurate statistics. As discussed earlier, many victims are afraid or unwilling to report abuse due to fear of their abuser, lack of trust in authorities, or a belief that nothing will be done to help them. This underreporting further obscures the true picture of domestic violence prevalence.

Despite these challenges, the available data, even if incomplete, paints a grim picture. In the United States, for example, intimate partner violence accounts for a staggering 15% of all violent crime. This means that nearly one in six violent crimes are committed within the supposed safety of intimate relationships.

The statistics also reveal that women between the ages of 18-24 are most commonly abused by an intimate partner. This is a particularly vulnerable age group, often facing financial dependence, social pressures, and a lack of experience in navigating unhealthy relationships.

Furthermore, the data shows that a staggering 1 in 4 women and 1 in 9 men experience severe intimate partner violence in their lifetime. These numbers are a stark reminder that domestic violence is not a gender-specific issue; it affects people of all genders, ages, and backgrounds.

While these statistics are difficult to confront, they serve a crucial purpose: they validate the experiences of countless victims and survivors, including my own. They demonstrate that my story is not an isolated incident, but rather a reflection of a widespread and deeply troubling reality.

By acknowledging the challenges in gathering accurate statistics and highlighting the available data, I hope to shed light on the global crisis of domestic violence. While the numbers may be incomplete, they provide a glimpse into the magnitude of the problem and underscore the urgent need for prevention, intervention, and support services for victims and survivors.

Last Note

My hope in sharing these statistics is not to sensationalize my story but to illuminate a pervasive issue that often remains hidden in the shadows. I want other survivors to know they are not alone, that their experiences are valid, and that healing is possible. By sharing my own journey, I hope to offer a beacon of hope to those who may feel lost in their own darkness.

Understanding the scope of domestic violence is the first step towards creating meaningful change. By acknowledging the prevalence of this issue, we can break the silence that allows it to thrive. We can challenge the stigma that prevents victims from seeking help and empower them to find the support they need.

I believe that knowledge is power. By sharing this research, I hope to educate and inform others about the realities of domestic violence. The more we understand about this issue, the better equipped we will be to prevent it, intervene when necessary, and provide support for those who have been affected.

My ultimate goal is to create a ripple effect of awareness and change. I hope that by sharing my story and the knowledge I've gained, others will feel that they have the power to speak out, to seek help, and to become advocates for a world free from violence.

I believe that together, we can make a difference. We can create a culture where victims are supported, abusers are held accountable, and violence is no longer tolerated. By sharing our stories, by raising our voices, and by working together, we can build a future where everyone feels safe, valued, and liberated.

If my mother were still alive, she would agree.

THE END.